# Howard Hawks

Known for creating classic films including *His Girl Friday*, *The Big Sleep*, *Bringing Up Baby*, and *Gentlemen Prefer Blondes*, Howard Hawks is one of the best-known Hollywood "auteurs," but the important role that music plays in his films has been generally neglected by film critics and scholars. In this concise study, Gregory Camp demonstrates how Hawks's use of music and musical treatment of dialogue articulate the group communication that is central to his films. In five chapters, Camp explores how the notion of "music" in Hawks's films can be expanded beyond the film score, and the techniques by which Hawks and his collaborators (including actors, screenwriters, composers, and editors) achieve this heightened musicality.

**Gregory Camp** is a Senior Lecturer at the University of Auckland School of Music, New Zealand.

**Filmmakers and Their Soundtracks**
Series Editor: James Wierzbicki
*The University of Sydney, Australia*

**Terrence Malick**
Sonic Style
*James Wierzbicki*

**Howard Hawks**
Music as Communication in Film
*Gregory Camp*

# Howard Hawks

Music as Communication in Film

**Gregory Camp**

Routledge
Taylor & Francis Group

NEW YORK AND LONDON

First published 2020
by Routledge
52 Vanderbilt Avenue, New York, NY 10017

and by Routledge
2 Park Square, Milton Park, Abingdon, Oxon, OX14 4RN

*Routledge is an imprint of the Taylor & Francis Group, an informa business*

© 2020 Taylor & Francis

*Library of Congress Cataloging-in-Publication Data*
A catalog record for this title has been requested

ISBN: 978-0-367-21160-8 (hbk)
ISBN: 978-0-367-48975-5 (pbk)
ISBN: 978-0-429-26577-8 (ebk)

Typeset in Times New Roman
by Wearset Ltd, Boldon, Tyne and Wear

# Contents

# Figures

# Series Foreword

The idea for a series of serious studies of various filmmakers' sonic styles began, as good ideas so often do, with a sidewalk conversation. In this case, the conversation took place during a break between sessions of the Music and the Moving Image conference at New York University in 2011; aside from the fresh air and coffee, its stimulus was the shared observation that since the conference's inception in 2007 there had been a subtle shift in the content of its papers. As one might expect from a conference named the way it is, most of the MaMI papers over the years indeed concentrated on music and its relationship to moving images, usually as demonstrated in singular examples of motion-picture art. But more and more, our sidewalk gang noted, attention was being focused not just on a particular film's music but on *all* its sonic elements, and not just on the sonic elements of a particular film but on the sonic elements of at least a number of films attributed to the same authorial source.

Thus was born *Music, Sound and Filmmakers: Sonic Style in Cinema* (Routledge, 2012), an edited collection whose dozen chapters deal succinctly yet comprehensively with the "stylish" use of sound by the film producers David O. Selznick and Val Lewton and the film directors Wes Anderson, Ingmar Bergman, the Coen brothers, Peter Greenaway, Krzystof Kiéslowski, Stanley Kubrick, David Lynch, Quentin Tarantino, Andrey Tarkovsky, and Gus Van Sant. In my Preface to that edited collection, I noted that "these twelve scholarly essays on sonic style in cinema represent only a first step on what surely will be a long path." A second step along this path, it surely seems, is Routledge's bold decision to follow up with not merely a sequel to the 2012 collection but with a series of monographs.

Contributors to the *Filmmakers and Their Soundtracks* series have been charged, as were the contributors to the 2012 collection, with two questions. Can you imagine a situation in which someone, arriving late to a showing of a film about which he or she has no advance information, might spontaneously say: "Ah, that *sounds* like a film by so-and-so?" If such a situation can indeed be imagined, then what is it about the film's sonic content that makes it attributable to one particular filmmaker? Like the essays in *Music, Sound and Filmmakers*, the books in the *Filmmakers and Their Soundtracks* series seek to answer that more difficult second question by explaining the many and complex reasons why a filmmaker's work, as a whole, has a distinct sonic "trademark."

James Wierzbicki
Series Editor

# Acknowledgments

First, I must thank my parents for introducing me both to music and to Classical Hollywood cinema from a very early age. With hindsight it seems inevitable that those twin passions would result in my first book. I have been lucky along the way to have had many excellent teachers, all of whom shaped my worldview and my writing, some in ways more directly related to the present work than others, but all important. There are too many to name here, but among my most important musical mentors as a university student were Karen Ahlquist, Robert Baker, Gisele Becker, and Douglas Boyce at George Washington University and Eric Clarke and Owen Rees at Oxford. I have been lucky to find a home at the University of Auckland School of Music, which hosts an extraordinarily supportive body of colleagues and students. Special thanks go to team musicology (Allan Badley, Davinia Caddy, Nancy November, Dean Sutcliffe, Peter Watts), the vocal/choral whānau (Morag Atchison, Rachel Fuller, Karen Grylls, Catrin Johnsson, Te Oti Rakena, Robert Wiremu), and the Music and Dance Library (Phillippa McKeown-Green and her expert team). Friends and colleagues at institutions all over the world have supported me and this work at various stages in diverse ways, especially Dan Blim, Michael Christoforidis, David Cosper, Peter Franklin, Sam Girling, Halvor Hosar, David Irving, Elizabeth Kertesz, David Larkin, Sam Owens, Graham Reid, Hamish Robb, Abi Sperling, Michael Weiss, Dave Wilson. Thanks to the students on whom I tried out some of the ideas presented herein in my Writing About Music, Music on Stage and Screen, Opera Scenes, and Jazz Research courses. And, finally, a big thanks to James Wierzbicki for commissioning this book.

# Introduction
## Howard Hawks's Sonic Style

Dean Martin and Ricky Nelson croon a cowboy song while John Wayne looks on admiringly. Lauren Bacall bounces to a Hoagy Carmichael tune with her newfound love Humphrey Bogart. A leopard becomes docile when it hears a venerable hit tune on a phonograph. Marilyn Monroe sings advice to women about the importance of precious stones. All these musical experiences appear in the films of a single Hollywood director, Howard Hawks (1896–1972). Popular among filmgoers and critics alike, Hawks is among the best-known of the Hollywood "auteurs," having been at the center of the discourse of most of the founding members of the both the French and Anglo-American auteur-structuralist schools of film criticism (such as Jacques Rivette, François Truffaut, Andrew Sarris, Peter Wollen, Robin Wood, Molly Haskell, and Peter Bogdanovich). But the important role that music plays in Hawks's films has been generally neglected by film critics and scholars; when they have looked at music it has mostly been to elucidate parts of individual films, rather than to see it as part of Hawks's style as a whole or as representative of the soundscapes of the times when the films were made. While it is well recognized that Hawks foregrounds group communication in his films, the plots of most of which involve the incorporation of an outsider into a group or the formation of a cohesive group from disparate individuals, it has gone largely unnoticed that in most of the films this group formation is articulated by music. For Hawks our notion of "music" must be expanded beyond a film score or diegetic songs, as he and his collaborators also use dialogue musically, carefully modulating its tempo and texture over the course of the films, as well as creating structures and formal styles that allude to music. When music as it is usually defined does appear in the films, Hawks tends to use it dialogically, as an explicit communication method rather than merely as affective underscoring of a scene's mood or as a way to create local color. In Hawks's world, most music is communication and most communication is musical, his films a compendium of the many ways in which people use music to communicate.

Howard Winchester Hawks was born in Goshen, Indiana, in 1896. Like many of his film director contemporaries, he ended up in Hollywood almost by chance, starting out as a mechanic and working his way rapidly up the chain of command to take on increasing responsibility within the burgeoning field of film-making. Working for the Fox Film Corporation, his first chances to direct came in the mid-1920s, and his busy career did not let up until a gradual retirement in the 1960s. He directed his final film, *Rio Lobo*, in 1970 and died in 1977. He was known in Hollywood as a laid-back director/producer who could work in practically any genre. Unlike many other directors, he was throughout most of his career also an independent producer, moving between studios according to the project he was working on. This means that he often had more control over his films than many of his colleagues could boast of, and this control allowed him to develop a distinctive sonic style within the standard production processes of the time.

Through case studies drawn from across Hawks's extensive oeuvre, this book explores the techniques by which the director and his collaborators (actors, screenwriters, composers, editors) achieve this heightened musicality. After an introduction that discusses Hawks's central position within film scholarship, along with the general place of music in his films and the films' place within Classical Hollywood musical practices, this book's five chapters will each delve into a particular way in which music is used in Hawks's films, and will each present a few specific case studies. Not all of Hawks's approximately 40 films will be analyzed in detail, but most merit at least some mention. In addition to his most famous films like *His Girl Friday* (1940) and *Rio Bravo* (1959), some of his lesser-known films, like *A Song is Born* (1948) and *Land of the Pharaohs* (1955), will be discussed in some depth because of the interesting music therein. Just because a film was not successful on its release or has not been subsequently re-appraised does not mean it is unworthy of discussion; unsuccessful films can still teach us a great deal about film-making practices and interesting reasons can sometimes be found for their very lack of success. In the case of Hawks, many of the unsuccessful films also feature unsuccessful uses of music, evidence of the importance of the film/music synergy that his most effective work embodies.

I come to this project as a Hawks fan. *Bringing Up Baby* (1938) has been a favorite film of mine since my childhood, long before I knew it as a "Howard Hawks" film and even longer before I ever thought I would become a film musicologist. It has, in fact, long been one of my "top three," along with *Sunset Boulevard* (1950) and *Vertigo* (1958) (heady stuff for a 12-year-old, but all notably musical films, so the writing on the screen was there). The next Hawks film I saw was probably *His Girl Friday* (approached as a Cary Grant fan), but it was not until my university years that I began to discover his entire oeuvre, and to notice the commonalities his films share. I rediscovered Hawks as part of a general binge of Classical Hollywood films during the completion of my doctorate, a genial way to distract one from the grind of thesis-writing. The doctorate was on Monteverdi, and it was not lost on me that the dramaturgical structures of early Venetian opera frequently mirror those of Classical Hollywood; as has often been stated, Hollywood film is opera presented through electronic media and writ large. While he never staged an opera, or indeed any "live" theatrical entertainment, Hawks's style is often operatic. He is primarily a director of ensembles, though, a Mozartian or Verdian director rather than a Handelian or Wagnerian one. His films do their narrative work by showing people communicating with each other through both music and words. He almost never used voiceovers and only rarely employed the large-scale musical scores that were popular throughout much of the period in which he worked. The music in his films is usually diegetic and of limited scale, and the dialogue is usually rapid and naturalistic. One can only imagine what he would have done with the intricacies of the Mozart/Da Ponte ensembles, or the Verdi/Boito ones, or even the Monteverdi/Busenello groupings of *L'incoronazione di Poppea*. The chapters of this book are arranged around these ensemble types – duets, choruses, and quartets – varied ensembles sometimes even implying that the audience should take part in the music-making as well.

Chapter 1, "Arranging an Ensemble," will explore the mechanisms in Hawks's films by which an outsider is incorporated into a cohesive group by musical means. Hawks takes for granted that part of being "good," worthy of respect and inclusion, is being musical. While he is often seen as a stereotypically masculine director reflective of mid-twentieth-century American attitudes toward gender, which usually place music firmly within the "feminine" sphere, the prominence of musical prowess as a marker of quality in his films makes us question this seeming status quo. In *Only Angels Have Wings* (1939), Bonnie (Jean Arthur) is the stereotypical "Hawksian woman" as she becomes one of the gang of intrepid airmen. She accomplishes this through her musical ability. In *Hatari!* (1962), another woman (Dallas, played by Elsa Martinelli) joins a group of male animal trappers by, like Bonnie, demonstrating her skills at the piano. This scene has been dismissed as self-plagiarism, but the different context of the scene lends it a different meaning. Conversely, in *Ball of Fire* (1941), the genders are swapped as Professor Potts (Gary Cooper) slowly comes around to the jazz music of Sugarpuss O'Shea (Barbara Stanwyck), only after his older colleagues have already succumbed to her and her music's charms.

Chapter 2, "Speaking a Duet," looks at Hawks's use of music on a more intimate scale. Hawks often treats dialogue as if it were music, casting his actors in such a way that their voices complement each other. In his romantic comedies (broadly defined) the characters' arguments and teasing eventually become markers of love. The connection between opera and cinema is especially strong in these films' use of dialogue, akin to the traditional operatic duet, translated to the new medium of the talking film. In *Twentieth Century* (1934), Oscar Jaffe and Lily Garland (John Barrymore and Carole Lombard) scream and shout at each other constantly, a type of relationship heightened even further in *His Girl Friday* with Walter Burns and Hildy Johnson (Cary Grant and Rosalind Russell). By careful vocal casting and a masterful use of rhythm, Hawks not only shows how these couples were made for each other, but lets us *hear* their compatibility. *The Big Sleep* (1946) was revised in post-production to capitalize on the real-life romance of stars Humphrey Bogart and Lauren Bacall; most of the changes consisted of adding dialogue scenes full of innuendo. The two actors' low voices complement each other so closely that the semantic content of their dialogues takes a back seat to their timbre as the characters' relationship develops.

In many of Hawks's films, male groups sing to demonstrate their solidarity and to reinforce their common goals. Chapter 3, "Singing a Chorus," explores these choral structures. Hawks's first sound film, *The Dawn Patrol* (1930), foregrounds music as World War I aviators sing with each other, not only to bring their group together but also to give voice to sentiments that they might not be comfortable expressing in speech. Music is used similarly in *Tiger Shark* (1932) and *The Big Sky* (1952), as group singing acts as a marker of the communities portrayed (Portuguese- and French-American, respectively). Hawks's most extensive use of the male chorus appears in two of his films scored by Dimitri Tiomkin, *Red River* (1948) and *Land of the Pharaohs* (1955), in which the chorus on the soundtrack stands in for the non-singing men we see working onscreen. The western *Red River* uses the harmonies of the chorus as a signifier and foreshadower of the ordering of American society staged by the film's narrative. In the historical epic *Land of the Pharaohs* the chorus represents simultaneously the voices of the enslaved masses and, due to the harmonic and rhythmic topics employed, the exotic "other." The voices we hear singing together in these films reinforce and musicalize Hawks's common narrative theme of group activity in pursuit of a common goal. These films also portray masculine societies founded upon music, again subtly interrogating the stereotypically "feminine" place of music in mid-twentieth-century America and offering an alternative vision of American masculinity.

Chapter 4, "Humming a Tune," examines those of Hawks's films in which music is marked as "music," rather than as a diegetic dramatic communication tool. In his two full-fledged musicals, *A Song Is Born* (1948) and *Gentlemen Prefer Blondes* (1953), the musical numbers engender a direct dialogue with the audience as the songs leave the screen and (the goal, at least) enter the minds of the audience so they will further engage with the songs in other performances, recordings, and sheet music. Similarly, Henry Mancini's hit "Baby Elephant Walk" from *Hatari!* acts as a detachable sellable tune. *Ball of Fire, To Have and Have Not,* and *The Big Sleep* feature diegetic performances of songs set off from the films' primary narrative thrust. The detachable musical numbers in these films bring the audience into dialogue: rather than merely watching musicians on screen, audience members are asked to engage with music as such, as they imagine themselves becoming part of the enjoyable communities they see on screen.

Chapter 5, "Barking a Quartet," returns to group formation through music-making. Hawks's most-discussed (and most-maligned) use of music is the song sequence in *Rio Bravo* (1959), which gives crooners Ricky Nelson and Dean Martin a chance to please their fans by singing. But the scene fits squarely into Hawks's wider project of group formation articulated by music. The quartet (Nelson, Martin, Walter Brennan, and John Wayne) in *Rio Bravo* is mirrored by an interspecies one in *Bringing Up Baby* (1938) – David, Susan, George the dog, and Baby the leopard – and another in *To Have and Have Not* – Bogart, Bacall, Brennan (again), and Hoagy Carmichael. In these films, collections of disparate individuals become cohesive groups by singing with each other. In *To Have and Have Not*, the stakes are especially high as the characters' journey into the French Resistance in Martinique is articulated by the ongoing composition of a song ("How Little We Know") across the length of the film. Music making becomes a marker of political resistance.

Finally, an appendix provides an annotated Howard Hawks filmography, with details of the musical elements of each film. Most of the existing books on Hawks end with filmographies that include other production details, which can also be found in standard resources like the Internet Movie Database and the AFI Catalogue of Feature Films; this filmography collates the musical material, information on which exists in disparate sources. It also provides a current (as of mid-2019) inventory of the commercial availability of the films. Some of Hawks's films have long been easy to find, first in prints available from film rental houses, then on VHS, then on DVD, Blu-Ray, and streaming services, while others remain stubbornly unreleased due to rights issues, problematic source material, or perceived lack of interest. All of Howard Hawks's films are of interest in that they share the director's signature, even though not all of them are equally successful. According to Andrew Sarris, "that one can discern the same directorial signature over a wide variety of genres is proof of artistry. That one can still enjoy the genres for their own sake is proof of the artist's professional urge to entertain."[1] Sarris, for whom Hawks was a "pantheon" director, takes an extreme point of view (which sometimes led him to consider his favorite directors' failures as better than lesser directors' successes), but what he says is certainly true of Hawks. The corpus of the director's 40-odd films serves both as an artistic testament and as a microcosm of Hollywood genre practices of the mid-twentieth century.

## Hawks in Film Scholarship

Any artist-focused work such as this must be carried out in dialogue with the critical and scholarly work already done on the artist. An expansive literature exists on Howard Hawks and his films, expertly detailed and annotated by Michael J. Anderson in his entry for *Oxford Bibliographies*, but few scholars have focused on music in Hawks's films.[2] The British Film Institute has published two major collections of essays on Hawks. The first, *Howard Hawks: American Artist*, edited by Jim Hillier and Peter Wollen, draws from a wide range of sources ranging from a 1928 French review of *A Girl in Every Port* to a 1996 essay by Laura Mulvey on *Gentlemen Prefer Blondes*.[3] That none of the 30 pieces in the collection make more than a passing reference to music is reflective of the general paucity of musicological approaches to film during the range of years represented. The BFI's 2016 collection, *Howard Hawks: New Perspectives*, edited by Ian Brookes, does contain two essays on music: a chapter on music in Hawks's westerns by Kathryn Kalinak, and one on jazz in Hawks's 1940s films by Brookes.[4] This reflects the growing role musicology has played within film studies in the two decades since the previous BFI collection, and most of the existing musicologically-informed work on Hawks dates from this more recent time. Some of this work takes sound studies, broadly defined, as its starting point: Lea Jacobs discusses dialogue in Hawks's 1930s films in a chapter in her *Film Rhythm After Sound*.[5] David Arnold studies the music in *Rio Bravo* from a queer theory perspective in "My Rifle, My Pony, and Feathers: Music and the Making of Men in Howard Hawks' *Rio Bravo*."[6] Chapters and articles like these offer some useful vocabulary, allowing the findings in this book to be placed within a scholarly community while still leaving plenty of room for new insights here and, I hope, elsewhere. Most of the work on music in Hawks has been about *To Have and Have Not* or *Rio Bravo* (both discussed in the two musicological essays in Brookes' collection). This is unsurprising as these two films are the ones that most obviously foreground music, *To Have and Have Not* as part of its mise-en-scène and attached to the star persona of Lauren Bacall, and *Rio Bravo* as a major plot point with music playing an important role in the character Dude's (Dean Martin) rehabilitation.[7]

At least 18 monographs have been published on Hawks and his films – 12 that discuss his whole career, two book-length interviews, and four short books on individual films in the BFI Film Classics series. Hawks's many interviews give valuable insights into his practice, although as a consummate storyteller anything he said is to be taken with a considerable grain of salt. Of the full career-covering monographs, seven are in English, three are in French (Hawks, with Hitchcock, has been central to French cinephilia since the 1950s), and two are in German. Three of these are especially valuable in their comprehensiveness and their influence on other studies of Hawks, and as such have major bearing on the present study: Todd McCarthy's magisterial *Howard Hawks: The Grey Fox of Hollywood*, is to date the only full biography of the director and stands as the biographical benchmark for any Hawksian.[8] McCarthy carefully sifts through the tall tales Hawks was fond of telling to separate the real from the invented, and he provides full background information on the planning, filming, and release of the films. Robin Wood's *Howard Hawks* (first published in 1969 and expanded in 1981 and again in 2006) was the first major critical study on Hawks and remains one of the most effective and influential.[9] From a literary-critical perspective inspired by the work of F.R. Leavis, Wood focuses on the group dynamics and the foregrounding of self-respect in the films. Gerald Mast's *Howard Hawks: Storyteller* is a detailed account of Hawks's dramaturgy, exploring how Hawks's films function narratively.[10] The present book hopes to expand on both of these critics' work, questioning what happens when music is added to the formulas presented by Wood and the dramatic structures outlined by Mast, against the biographical and production background described by McCarthy. Wood and Mast do make some room in their books for music, recognizing the role music plays in creating Hawks's group structures, but I hope here to push their concepts further with the insights musicology can offer.

Hawks has been central to film scholarship more broadly, both in the Sarris-influenced auteur-structuralist school mentioned above and in neoformalist studies ranging from David Bordwell, Kristin Thompson, and Janet Staiger's seminal *The Classical Hollywood Cinema* through Bordwell's other writing (he has a special interest in *His Girl Friday*) and work by his followers.[11] Hawks also has pride of place in most introductory film textbooks and other overviews of film aesthetics and history.[12] The critical consensus, then, is that Howard Hawks is undeniably a central figure in the history of world cinema. This centrality is mirrored in the availability of the films themselves. Nearly all of Hawks's sound films have been released on DVD, sometimes in elaborate special editions, and many of the others are available to stream online (see the Appendix for details on these releases). Soundtrack recordings have been released for many of the films, notably a re-recording of the *Rio Bravo* score and releases of *The Big Sky*, *Rio Bravo*, and *Hatari!* that include alternate takes and other archival material. While a great deal of scholarly work has been done on Hawks (and after a lull in the 1990s and 2000s he seems to be making a comeback in scholarly discourse) there is ample room for a study of his films from a musicological perspective.

Hawks has served, along with John Ford, Alfred Hitchcock, and a few select others, as a primary touchstone for the auteurist school of film scholarship. Broadly defined, auteurism refers to a school of thought that places film directors at the center of critical work, seeing the director as the primary author of the filmic text. Peter Wollen's foundational *Signs and Meaning in the Cinema* centers largely on Hawks and Ford, and Andrew Sarris places Hawks in his "panthcon" of grcat American auteurs.[13] The French critics of *Cahiers du Cinéma* who first developed the *politique* of auteurist discourse placed Hawks at the center as well, evidenced by Jacques Rivette's famous 1956 essay "The Genius of Howard Hawks."[14] As soon as it emerged as a critical approach, auteurism was roundly criticized for placing its emphasis purely on the figure of the director, allegedly at the expense of other collaborators on the films and other ways of examining them. Yet we are stuck with auteurism whether we like it or not – look at any library shelves, any film festival, any database or catalog. Some of the studies of Hawks mentioned above fall into auteurist traps, especially the wide-ranging ones like Wood's monograph or Wollen's chapters. As acute as their critical faculties are, both scholars make assumptions of Hawks's direct involvement where subsequent research like McCarthy's has shown he was not actually involved. Writing as they were in the late 1960s, this is before the authors could argue away such things as being products of the "author function" (Foucault and Barthes not really becoming forces in Anglo-American criticism until the 1970s), and even subsequent revisions of the books have retained this hardline auteurist discourse, claiming that a real auteur should be assigned anything unique and artistic about the films. The rest, Wollen says, is "noise."[15] Gerald Mast is on firmer ground in his study *Howard Hawks Storyteller*, as he limits his purview to Hawks's role as screenwriter and/or dramaturg. Documentary evidence does exist for Hawks's intensive involvement with his films' screenplays, and Mast's account is grounded in such evidence. When the evidence runs out Mast uses interpretive strategies that still recognize Hawks as a collaborator in his films' storytelling. The more recent Hawks studies, such as those in Brookes' collection, limit their sights further by choosing topics for which sound interpretations can be made, as opposed to the Wood/Wollen approach which tries to take in everything about the oeuvre simultaneously. While many of the insights of the auteurist school remain valuable, most scholars have ceased using the term itself and have moved on from its problematic assumptions.

The wider corpus of film musicology offers many useful insights for the study of Hawks's sonic style. For an understanding of how the sonic and the visual come together in film my departure point is Michel Chion's work, which is most comprehensively summarized in *Film: A Sound Art*.[16] A number of other monographs have examined the sonic style of film directors and offer useful models for this mode of enquiry, including Kate McQuiston on Stanley Kubrick and Gayle Sherwood Magee on Robert Altman.[17] It is notable that Kubrick and Altman both emerged during the heyday of New Hollywood auteur-driven cinema, and that very little work has sought to connect earlier directors to a consistent musical style (two notable exceptions being on John Ford and Alfred Hitchcock).[18] This is partly because of the changes in Hollywood's production practices: directors simply had less control over music in the 1930s–1950s than they did in later decades. Hawks's position as a producer-director was rare in this period.[19]

The present study limits itself to Hawks's use of music (broadly defined), but placing this limit within an filmmaker-centered context causes an intriguing paradox to arise: unlike with his work on screenwriting (as Mast demonstrates), the documentary evidence often goes *against* the assumption that Hawks involved himself directly with his films' music. He often let go of his films once they left the soundstage, playing a less active role in their editing, scoring, and distribution than he did in their planning and shooting. This study therefore cannot be about *only* Hawks the singular artist, because Hawks sometimes demonstrably did not control the music in his films. But the fact that Hawks did not always have the last word over the music should not stop us from examining his films as a coherent set of musical texts. As an independent producer for most of his career, Hawks indeed offers an excellent opportunity for comparison of music across Hollywood studios. For a counterexample, if one were to look at music in Michael Curtiz's films one would be looking just as much at the use of music at the Warner Brothers studio, and to look at Douglas Sirk would be to look at Universal. That the way Hawks uses music is so consistent shows that he did indeed have an authorial (or at least "producerial") style. But studying the music in Hawks's films also allows us to point out interesting differences between studios and composers. The five westerns he directed are a case in point: the first three were all scored by Dimitri Tiomkin, *Red River* and *The Big Sky* in (on the surface at least) the traditional Hollywood mode and *Rio Bravo* transitional to 1960s scoring practices. *El Dorado* (Nelson Riddle, 1967) and *Rio Lobo* (Jerry Goldsmith, 1970) both have fairly standard and somewhat dull 1960s scores. Further research might demonstrate that Hawks, Hitchcock, and Ford were not the only musically astute directors in Hollywood, but for now it appears that these three directors were the exceptions that prove the rule.[20]

## A Brief History of Hawksian Music

With a directing career spanning from 1926 to 1970, Hawks worked through most of the major paradigm shifts in the uses of film music in Hollywood. The body of this book will explore synchronically various motifs that his work has in common, but first a general overview of Hawks's films' place within the history of film music will place his career into context. Hawks's long career both conforms to and departs from the typical use of music in Hollywood cinema during those 44 years.[21] That frequently repeated musical tropes are so often found in his work is a testament to Hawks's status as an artist. Most major mid-twentieth-century directors with equivalently long careers do not show such consistency in the way they use music. William Wyler's films, for example, conform much more strongly to the standards of musical dramaturgy that surrounded their production at specific times in specific studios, attentive as Wyler often was to the effects of music on his storytelling. The score of 1942's *Mrs. Miniver*, one of Wyler's biggest hits, is credited to Herbert Stothart but is in reality a classic example of

MGM's collective scoring practices at the time; the studio used its large stable of composers, orchestrators, and arrangers as a collective and without cue sheets it is difficult to attribute a particular cue to a specific composer, working as they all did in the MGM house style.[22] Wyler, as befitting his status as a major director, often attracted excellent and important scores for his later films as his reputation grew and the studios moved away from the earlier collaborative models, but the scores tend to be remembered as being connected with the films themselves more than with Wyler. The scores for Hawks's films are not of the type that appear on concert programs, unlike those of Wyler's *Ben-Hur* (Miklós Rózsa, 1959), *The Big Country* (Jerome Moross, 1958), or *The Heiress* (Aaron Copland, 1949). The only Hawks score that has been re-recorded in full is Tiomkin's *Red River* (by the Moscow Symphony Orchestra for Naxos). Michael Curtiz's work provides another example of standard practices of the time: note the popularity and importance of the scores of *The Adventures of Robin Hood* (1938) and *Casablanca* (1942), often remembered more as Erich Wolfgang Korngold and Max Steiner scores, respectively, than as Curtiz films. Conversely, the Alfred Hitchcock/Bernard Herrmann collaborations provide a case where film, director, and score lend each other celebrity. Yet Hawks's films do not have detachable scores like Herrmann's for Hitchcock. Nor are the scores for Hawks's films very showy, even when composers with recognizable and difficult-to-subordinate styles were working for him: compare Franz Waxman's intense scores working with Billy Wilder on *Sunset Boulevard* (1950) or George Stevens on *A Place in the Sun* (1951) with his minimal but effective scores for *To Have and Have Not* and *Air Force* (1943). Dimitri Tiomkin is the one exception to this, writing Hawks's most substantial scores, but this manner of scoring appears in only a small portion of his output.

Coming at the end of the "silent" era, Hawks's first films are standard examples of the late form of that style. As was common at that time, his films make frequent visual reference to music and sound, encouraging the audience to "hear" the films they are seeing, with the support of the musicians accompanying the film screening. Hawks's first major success, *A Girl in Every Port* (1928), features a memorable scene in which the two male protagonists "meet cute" and then have a fight in a typically Hawksian bar in the presence of musicians. Hawks gets a joke out of them: while the men are fighting, the band continues playing their instruments regardless, even as the men run into them. His last three silent films, *Fazil* (1928), *The Air Circus* (1928), and *Trent's Last Case* (1929), featured synchronized scores and sound effects that could be sent out to theaters outfitted with the new sound reproduction equipment. The only one of these films that is fully extant is *Fazil*, which Chapter 4 will show is a representative example of films made during this transitional period in its use of music, specifically song-plugging.

Hawks's earliest sound films are also typical of this time in Hollywood in their very limited use of music.[23] His first talkie, *The Dawn Patrol* (1930), which will be discussed more fully in Chapter 3, is typical in that non-diegetic music is heard only twice in the whole film, under the opening and closing credits. The film does, however, make extensive use of source music in a manner that will become typically Hawksian: music (here, the song "Poor Butterfly") runs through the film and articulates the narrative on a metaphorical plane. *The Crowd Roars* (1932) is the least musical of all Hawks's films. Aside from the opening credits (and then only after the sound of racing cars has been established) and a tiny snippet of marching band music in the middle, no music is heard at all. Even the end credits are void of music; instead, we hear only the siren of the ambulance taking the protagonist, busted up in a car crash, to the hospital. In *Tiger Shark* (1932), underscore is used for the first time in a Hawks film: mandolins are heard playing when Portuguese fisherman Silva (Edward G. Robinson) talks to his daughter. While we could imagine an offscreen band here, that the music is carefully timed to the progression of the scene indicates that it is non-diegetic, as does the return of the same music when Silva proposes to his beloved Quita. *Viva Villa!* (1934) is the earliest film Hawks was directly involved in that features more substantial underscore throughout, with MGM's Herbert Stothart writing to the model Max Steiner was developing at RKO. Notably, *Viva Villa!* also credits a "musical consultant," Juan Aguilar, who presumably oversaw the use of Mexican folk music in the film. The rest of the 1930s films vary between fully underscored projects (usually dramas like *Barbary Coast* [1935] and *Come and Get It* [1936], both with scores by Alfred Newman) and those with very little score (usually comedies like *Twentieth Century* [1934] and *Bringing Up Baby* [1938]), matching the general genre/music trends of the decade. Most of these films do give music some narrative importance whether it is diegetic or non-diegetic, and it is in this that Hawks's films are set apart from those of his contemporaries. In addition, Hawks's careful use of dialogue as sound recording technology improved also has an important role to play in the sonic profiles of his films.

By the 1940s the musical language of underscore was fully established and most films featured it to some extent, sometimes approaching the "saturation score" with music playing throughout. Usually Hawks avoided the overuse of underscore in his 1940s films, although *Sergeant York* (1941) (perhaps significantly not a project developed by Hawks himself) has a very expansive score by Max Steiner. In *To Have and Have Not* (1944) and *The Big Sleep* (1946), both films with a great deal of music of various types, underscore alternates with featured diegetic music. *Red River* (1948), whose score by Dimitri Tiomkin was the biggest to date for a Hawks film, ushers in the more epic mode of filmmaking that Hawks would experiment with throughout the 1950s. The 1950s was Hawks's Tiomkin decade, and Tiomkin most often worked on an expansive canvas. Aside from the comedies *I Was a Male War Bride* (1949) and *Monkey Business* (1952), and the musicals *A Song is Born* (1948) and *Gentlemen Prefer Blondes* (1953), all of Hawks's films between 1948 and 1959 have Tiomkin scores (*Red River*, *The Thing from Another World* [1951], *The Big Sky* [1952], *Land of the Pharaohs* [1955], and *Rio Bravo* [1959]). The last, *Rio Bravo*, is especially interesting musically, combing a large-scale score with frequent dramatic use of diegetic music. This was the most consistent musical partnership in Hawks's filmmaking career, although it had run its course by the end of the decade. Hawks has originally planned to use Tiomkin for *Hatari!* (1962), but Tiomkin was not interested in using the native African instruments that Hawks wanted for the score.

Hawks's hiring of Henry Mancini for *Hatari!* ushers in a new phase in Hollywood film scoring, one with a rather more diffuse use of music and increasing influence from popular music rather than the orchestral sound world. Mancini (two films) and Nelson Riddle (two films) were leading exponents of this newer style, although aside from *Hatari!*, which approaches the earlier films in its musical apparatus, their work for Hawks was somewhat lackluster. It seems appropriate that Hawks's final film, *Rio Lobo* (1970), was scored by Jerry Goldsmith, who would become a leading exponent of the next generation's return to the more orchestral style of the past after writing arguably more experimental scores in the 1960s.

Over the course of Hawks's long career we can see the outline of the history of standard Hollywood music practices: synchronized scores for late silent films, the turn away from music in the early sound era, the standardization of underscoring practices in the mid-1930s and 1940s, the saturation scores in the epic 1950s, and the influence of popular music and the turn away from the symphony orchestra in the 1960s. Only Alfred Hitchcock had a similar career trajectory, albeit slightly different in its first half due to his presence in England until 1940: music only "as needed" in the 1930s, the watershed of Franz Waxman's score for *Rebecca* in 1940, then leading to Bernard Herrmann's epic 1950s scores (albeit epic in a very different way from Tiomkin's scores for Hawks), lackluster 1960s scores, and finally a score by an up-and-comer – in Hitchcock's case, John Williams, writing for *Family Plot* (1976). Unlike Hitchcock, though, Hawks was consistently committed to the dramatic use of diegetic music throughout his career. After 1930s films like *The Man Who Knew Too Much* (1934) and *The Lady Vanishes* (1938), Hitchcock turned away from this musical storytelling mode, preferring by the time he developed his partnership with Herrmann to use primarily underscore rather than onscreen musical performance to help tell his stories. Musically, it is here that these two great filmmakers set themselves apart from each other; Hawks is, in fact, the only Hollywood director regularly to use this mode. This is what makes his films such fascinating source material for the film musicologist.

# Notes

1 Andrew Sarris, *The American Cinema: Directors and Directions* (New York: Dutton, 1968), 56.
2 Michael J. Anderson, "Howard Hawks," in *Oxford Bibliographies* (Oxford University Press Online, 2011), http://oxfordbibliographies.com.
3 Jim Hillier and Peter Wollen, eds., *Howard Hawks: American Artist* (London: British Film Institute, 1996).
4 Ian Brookes, ed., *Howard Hawks: New Perspectives* (London: British Film Institute, 2016).
5 Lea Jacobs, *Film Rhythm After Sound* (Berkeley: University of California Press, 2015).
6 David Arnold, "My Rifle, My Pony, and Feathers: Music and the Making of Men in Howard Hawks' *Rio Bravo*," *Quarterly Review of Film and Video* 23, no. 3 (2006): 267–279.
7 On *To Have and Have Not*, see also David Neumeyer and James Buhler, *Meaning and Interpretation of Music in Cinema* (Bloomington: University of Indiana Press, 2015) and David Neumeyer, James Buhler, and Rob Deemer, *Hearing Through Movies: Music and Sound in Film History* (New York: Oxford University Press, 2010).
8 Todd McCarthy, *Howard Hawks: The Grey Fox of Hollywood* (New York: Grove Press, 1997).
9 Robin Wood, *Howard Hawks* (Detroit: Wayne State University Press, 2006).
10 Gerald Mast, *Howard Hawks, Storyteller* (New York: Oxford University Press, 1982).
11 David Bordwell, Kirstin Thompson, and Janet Staiger, *The Classical Hollywood Cinema: Film Style and Mode of Production to 1960* (New York: Columbia University Press, 1985).
12 These are too numerous to provide a comprehensive list here, but see for example the frequent passing references to Hawks in Robert Kolker, *Film, Form, and Culture* (New York: McGraw Hill, 2006) and the many Hawks case studies in Todd Berliner, *Hollywood Aesthetic: Pleasure in American Cinema* (New York: Oxford University Press, 2017).
13 Peter Wollen, *Signs and Meaning in the Cinema*, 3rd ed. (London: British Film Institute, 2013); Sarris, *The American Cinema*.
14 Anthologized in Hillier and Wollen, *Howard Hawks: American Artist*.
15 Wollen, *Signs and Meaning in the Cinema*, 105.
16 Chion, Michel. *Film: A Sound Art*, trans. Claudia Gorbman (New York: Columbia University Press, 2009).
17 Kate McQuiston, *We'll Meet Again: Musical Design in the Films of Stanley Kubrick* (New York: Oxford University Press, 2013); Gayle Sherwood Magee, *Altman's Soundtracks: Film, Music and Sound from "M\*A\*S\*H" to "A Prairie Home Companion"* (New York: Oxford University Press, 2014).
18 Kathryn Kalinak, *How the West Was Sung: Music in the Westerns of John Ford* (Berkeley: University of California Press, 2007); Jack Sullivan, *Hitchcock's Music* (New Haven, CT: Yale University Press, 2006).
19 Nathan Platte explores the role producer David O. Selznick played in developing the music of his films in *Making Music in Selznick's Hollywood* (New York: Oxford University Press, 2018). The director is not necessarily the only musical artist (including composers, still under-studied) that needs to be explored in this period. Many of these scholars' work also appears in the seminal collection *Music,*

*Sound and Filmmakers: Sonic Style in Cinema*, ed. James Wierzbicki (New York: Routledge, 2012).

20 French classical cinema might offer further avenues for exploration, especially Jean Vigo, René Clair, and Marcel Carné, who had idiosyncratic views on music in film. Michel Chion has begun to explore this area in *La musique au cinéma* (Paris: Fayard, 1995), work continued by Hannah Lewis in *French Musical Culture and the Coming of Sound Cinema* (New York: Oxford University Press, 2019).

21 The most comprehensive histories of Hollywood film music are James Wierzbicki, *Film Music: A History* (New York: Routledge, 2009) and Mervyn Cooke, *A History of Film Music* (Cambridge: Cambridge University Press, 2008).

22 Witness André Previn's recollections of his early years working in the MGM music department in the late 1940s in *No Minor Chords: My Days in Hollywood* (New York: Doubleday, 1991).

23 For a detailed history of the use of music in this transitional period, see Michael Slowik, *After the Silents: Hollywood Film Music in the Early Sound Era, 1926–1934* (New York: Columbia University Press, 2014).

# 1    Arranging an Ensemble

The auteurist critics discussed in the Introduction find that Hawks's most defining narrative preoccupation is staging group activity directed toward a common goal. Some of his films feature already established groups, others are about newly forming groups, and others, to be discussed in this chapter, center on an outsider who is incorporated into a group. Hawks often uses music as a symbol of that incorporation, and such is the case in *Only Angels Have Wings* (1939), *Hatari!* (1962), and *Ball of Fire* (1942). In all three films, a female protagonist uses music to work her way into an established ensemble, and the newcomer changes that group's identity.

## Ensembles in the Andes: *Only Angels Have Wings*

*Only Angels Have Wings* is the story of a group of American aviators who run a mail courier service in the fictional South American port of Barranca. They are led by Geoff Carter (Cary Grant), the most intrepid of them all, who only flies when it is too dangerous for anyone else to go aloft. His sidekick and best friend is Kid Dabb (Thomas Mitchell), and the group uses a bar managed by Dutchy (Sig Ruman) as their headquarters. Importantly, the bar (like so many of the bars in Hawks's films) has a piano and a house band. Bonnie Lee (Jean Arthur), an American fresh off the boat in Barranca, meets two pilots at the dock and accompanies them to Dutchy's bar for a steak dinner. As soon as they arrive, one of the pilots, Joe (Noah Beery Jr.), is called on a job through bad weather and is killed in a crash during his attempted return. Bonnie is confused and horrified by the other men's easy acceptance of Joe's death, and especially by Geoff who sits down to eat Joe's unfinished steak. The men are seemingly cruel in their initiation of Bonnie into their way of thinking, asking her, "Who's Joe?" when she wants to talk about the dead pilot. The men sing the Spanish–American War song "Break the News to Mother" (composed by Charles K. Harris in 1897) to mock what they perceive as Bonnie's naivety and sentimentality, flaunting their ability to look death in the face and laugh at soft-heartedness. Outraged at their flippancy, Bonnie storms out of the bar in tears. She quickly realizes, however, that she reacted inappropriately to the men's actions, feeling embarrassed by her sentimentality (a traditionally "female" quality in the macho context of 1939 Hollywood, and one that Hawks was fond of questioning). As she speaks to the other airmen about Geoff, Bonnie very quickly takes on the mantle of a quintessential Hawksian woman, deciding to "toughen up" and join the men on their own terms.[1] When Bonnie reenters the bar, Geoff is attempting to lead the group in Shelton Brooks' 1910 hit "Some of These Days," but he keeps playing an incorrect chord on the piano, E-flat major where it should be E minor. Bonnie goes to the instrument to correct the chord and then sits down to lead the group herself. She impresses the assembled crowd of airmen and local musicians and their girlfriends, going on to suggest that they play Moisés Simons' 1928 hit "The Peanut Vendor." By the time the scene fades out our impression is that Bonnie is now ingrained into the group and their way of thinking.

Bonnie's newfound centrality in the group is emphasized by Hawks's *mise-en-scène* throughout this sequence: first, the camera follows Bonnie as she reenters the bar (Figure 1.1), says a friendly "hello" to some of the customers, and walks over to the piano, at which Geoff is already seated.

*Figure 1.1* Bonnie confidently enters the bar.
Source: *Only Angels Have Wings.*

By having the camera travel with her, keeping her centered in the frame, Hawks makes it clear that Bonnie has a newfound control over the space. The only previous substantial tracking shot in this section of the film followed Geoff (who, like Bonnie, moved from the right side of the room to the left) as he joined his colleagues and Bonnie at their table. That shot crowned Jeff as the dominant character in the bar, and this following one allows Bonnie to take an analogous position. Next, Bonnie gives the other musicians instructions and sits at the piano in the center of the shot, closely surrounded by the fliers and their friends, who form a protective halo around her. The shot is very crowded at the beginning of the scene, and becomes more so as other denizens of the bar gather around Bonnie as she continues playing (Figure 1.2). By presenting such a crowded shot Hawks emphasizes the self-sufficiency of the microcosm represented by this South American bar: nothing outside of the shot matters in this moment of musical performance. Because all of the sounds we hear find their source in the shot itself, it forms an autonomous audiovisual world (pace Michel Chion, there *is* a soundtrack, at least in this shot).[2] Geoff is clearly surprised, impressed, and aroused by Bonnie's skill – "hello, professional," he says. Unlike Geoff, the audience already has a feeling for Bonnie's musicality, as at the very beginning of the film she sang

*Figure 1.2* Bonnie shows off her pianistic skills.
Source: *Only Angels Have Wings.*

along with a group of street singers, to the delight of the natives. Although Jean Arthur as Bonnie is the "star" in this scene, Cary Grant's performance is also notable in its subtlety as he supports his co-star.

Hawks breaks up this sequence with a brief medium shot of Bonnie playing, reminding the audience that the scene is about Bonnie, cueing us to focus on her realization of how she can fit into the group (Figure 1.3). This happens when Geoff gives her a drink, which she sips while continuing to play. She is lit frontally so that our gaze gravitates toward her. When the song finishes, Bonnie begins absent-mindedly to play "Break the News to Mother," a momentary lapse in her newfound ability to ignore death, the music seeming to speak from her subconscious, but when she and Geoff simultaneously notice what she is playing she breaks off (Geoff: "Who's Joe?" Bonnie: "Never heard of him."). It also allows the two a more intimate moment as they share this shot equally, foreshadowing the fact (in case we didn't already know it) that they will fall in love. Bonnie immediately breaks the awkward mood by asking if anyone knows "The Peanut Vendor," which all eagerly strike up, Bonnie playing the piano and Geoff singing (Figure 1.4). Although very similar to the previous group shot, the angle of this new shot is subtly different, placing both Bonnie and Geoff in the middle of the frame (compare

*Figure 1.3* Bonnie settles in with a drink.

Source: *Only Angels Have Wings.*

Figures 1.2 and 1.4) and allowing us to see them both more clearly. In "Some of these Days" Bonnie was the musician and Geoff was part of the audience, but in "The Peanut Vendor" they both participate as equal partners in the musical group. Could they do anything next but fall in love?

The music-making continues into the next scene, still set in the bar but after an ellipsis of time is indicated by a fade-out and a shot of the bar's clock. There is a dissolve from the clock to a medium shot of Bonnie alone at the piano playing Liszt's "Liebestraum." She is clearly very much at home now, having made the piano her own, as she provides a melancholic diegetic accompaniment for the subsequent scene in which Geoff and the others discuss what to do with the dead Joe's belongings. Aside from one further scene in the bar in which music is playing, no other music is heard until the final sequence of the film, where nondiegetic strings accompany Kid's death scene (Kid having been injured in a dramatic flight through a storm over the Andes). Using underscore in this scene feels like a miscalculation, especially since there has been no other underscoring since the film's opening credits. Although Dimitri Tiomkin's music here is unobtrusive, it adds a veneer of sentimentality that the scene does not need: everything in the film prior to this point has told us that this is one of the most unsentimental groups of men ever

*Figure 1.4* Geoff sings "The Peanut Vendor."
Source: *Only Angels Have Wings.*

to grace the screen. Hawks has set us up to feel like Geoff did when Bonnie started to play "Break the News to Mother:" we have been conditioned by the foregoing not to accept that the group would go in for this sort of sentimental affect. The equivalent scene (the death of another airman) in Hawks's 1943 film *Air Force* is more effective because Franz Waxman's music is dissonant and eerie rather than sentimental, and more underscore is used throughout the film so it does not come so unexpectedly. In *Only Angels Have Wings*, the group has been established as musically self-sufficient: they do not need sentimental underscoring to function as a cohesive group, and the music for Geoff's farewell to Kid strikes a note of sentimentality that Bonnie has already learned is not appropriate for these men.

The final music in *Only Angels Have Wings* is heard shortly thereafter: the popular 1925 Marcos Jiménez song "Adiós Mariquita Linda," sung by Manuel Álvarez Maciste accompanying himself on his guitar. Bonnie sits at the piano at the center of the shot but does not play (Figure 1.5). This shot is visually the opposite of the earlier one, filmed from the other side of the piano, creating a balanced form between these two music scenes. Rather than everyone participating, they all listen to the singer with a sense of melancholy about Kid's death. Bonnie is now one of the group of listeners; having proven

*Figure 1.5* Mourning for Kid.
Source: *Only Angels Have Wings.*

herself to be a capable performer, she has been accepted by the group and has no need to show off. Importantly, this is music as performance instead of music as participation: listening to someone else give voice to their grief seems to help the airmen to process it. Unlike in Kid's death scene, the music here is still part of the world of the bar: it shows the complexity of this bar as a place for "musicking," a place for both participatory and listening-based modes of performance.[3] Maciste's performance is melancholic yet void of the overdetermined sentimentality of a song like "Break the News to Mother." Suddenly a new mail call comes in that snaps the group out of their melancholy. The volume and tempo of the voices pick up, leading into the final bit of jaunty underscore and the film's inevitable happy ending.

In his monograph on Hawks, Leland Poague sees the two singing scenes – the scene on the dock at the beginning of the film and the one in the bar – as "primarily female," as compared to the masculine affordances of the professional aviation outfit.[4] But the musicking could instead be seen in a way that deconstructs the male/female dichotomy, as both genders participate musically in both scenes. The native musicians are primarily male, men and women listening and singing along, and the airmen form a primarily homosocial musical society until Bonnie joins them, but in both cases the musical product comes from both genders. One might argue that the natives' "otherness" mirrors a female otherness (and that the natives are feminized), so that when Bonnie sings along with them she is only an other joining another group of others, with a hint of the trope of the Western woman forcing herself upon the natives' way of life.[5] This post-colonial reading would be hard to argue with, but the scene in the bar is more ideologically complex. When she leads the men in "Some of these Days," Bonnie's musical expertise shines through, although they were doing well enough without her aside from that single pesky chord (and indeed play perfectly well without her at other points in the film), so we cannot really speak of the female influence allowing better music to be made. The other musicians, and Geoff, take the lead in the following "Peanut Vendor," Bonnie now playing the piano as part of the ensemble rather than as its leader. On whose terms does Bonnie make music with the men? First, she plays a dominant, then a supporting role in the musical group, and Geoff is happy to take the opposite role, only listening in "Some of these Days" and leading in "The Peanut Vendor." This sharing of power within the relationship is undermined as the plot soon becomes a conventional love triangle when Rita Hayworth turns up in the role of Geoff's ex-flame, then with Geoff deciding on her behalf whether Bonnie should stay with him in Barranca. But this important early scene of musical performance seems to offer a brief vision of more equal gender relationships, a type of relationship also hinted at in *Bringing Up Baby* (1938) and to be expanded upon in *To Have and Have Not* (1944) (to be discussed in Chapter 4). Although he is certainly not a feminist in his working life, Geoff is quite willing to relinquish musical power to a woman who shows herself to have more talent than he. The gender and musical dynamics here are more complex than Poague, Haskell, and other critics of this film have given Hawks and his collaborators credit for; if only the rest of the film bore out the promise of this scene. Poague is partly correct to say that with Hawks "it is usually the case, as in *Only Angels*, that women are quite readily accepted into the group by everyone *except* the ostensible hero, and his refusal either to accept the woman or to acknowledge her sexual integrity reflects generally upon the hero's insufficiency, not hers";[6] while the film as a whole bears this observation out, the song scene undermines it, as it is clear that Geoff is quite happy for Bonnie to sing. In addition, Cary Grant is willing here to display a type of masculinity very different from most of 1939's screen men: his reaction to Jean Arthur's playing is worlds away from *Gone with the Wind*'s Rhett Butler's demanded dominance over Scarlett O'Hara, or from the Ringo Kid's absolute power over the mise-en-scène of *Stagecoach*. Hawks's many musical men should make us question the supposedly traditional place of music within the female sphere, especially during the Classical Hollywood period.[7]

## Hanging Out in Africa: *Hatari!*

The scene of group musical performance that is so central to *Only Angels Have Wings* is revisited in 1962's *Hatari!*, now with Elsa Martinelli in the Jean Arthur role and Hardy Krüger in Cary Grant's. Like *Only Angels Have Wings*, *Hatari!* is set among a group of expatriates involved in a dangerous, exciting business in an exotic location, here trapping animals on the African savannah for zoos in Europe and America. Also like the earlier film, most of the action takes place in a "home" compound, here the trappers' lodge that, like all good Hawksian public spaces, features a prominent bar. German trapper Kurt (Krüger) attempts to play "Swanee River" on the bar's piano but keeps playing a wrong note; photographer Dallas (Martinelli) steps in to correct him, then fellow trapper and comic relief Pockets (Red Buttons) joins them on his harmonica.

The outline of the 1962 scene is strikingly similar to the 1939 version, down to the dialogue: "You'd better be good," says Kurt, the same thing Jeff said to Bonnie when she corrected his wrong chord and sat down to play. The dynamic here is rather different from *Only Angels Have Wings*, however, as these two characters are not going to fall in love. Instead, the focus is squarely on Dallas's integration into the group of trappers. Dallas is a photographer who has been hired to shoot a story about Sean Mercer's (John Wayne) animal trapping business in Africa, and it is not Krüger's character Kurt she falls in love with but rather Mercer/Wayne himself, whose persona throughout his mature career is decidedly unmusical. Aside from the different dramatic context, is this scene any more than a case of Hawksian self-plagiarism?

Dallas is not a musician as Bonnie is (although she does noodle at the piano at one point later in the film), so her expertise in the "Swanee River" scene seems somewhat arbitrary. But the scene's existence is a testament to Hawks's continuing predilection for using music as a plot device and it is clearly a watershed moment for Dallas, who from this scene on becomes a firm part of the group.

The "Swanee River" scene is not the only re-worked musical device from an earlier film that appears in *Hatari!* Early in the film we see the male trappers drunkenly singing "Whiskey Leave Me Alone" with each other over their truck radios on the way back from a night out. There is a link here to *The Big Sky* (1952), where Western traders Jim and Boone (Kirk Douglas and Dewey Martin) sing the same song together in a saloon. Drinking and music often come together in Hawks's world for the purposes of male bonding. As early as *The Dawn Patrol* (1930), the characters sing "Apple to Plum" while drunk.[8] As has been well established in the critical literature, and as even an uncritical appraisal of his films demonstrates, Hawks was fond of replaying his favorite devices over and over, especially in his later films. Rather than being merely derivative, these are instances of a master storyteller who knows a good trick and is not above repeating something that has been proven to work. The director's detractors see this sort of thing as evidence of his rapidly declining sense of originality late in his career, but his apologists, especially those who wrote for *Cahiers du Cinéma*, who adored *Hatari! because* of these echoes, see such repetitions as quintessential to Hawks's status as an auteur.

*Hatari!* is a typical example of what Quentin Tarantino labels the "hangout film" (even more so than *Rio Bravo*, his primary example), and music often has an important role to play in such films. In a post-screening talk about *Rio Bravo* at the 2007 Cannes Film Festival, Tarantino describes this genre: "There are certain movies that you hang out with the characters so much that they actually become your friends."[9] People often share music when hanging out in real life as a way to bond with each other, so it makes sense that the groups on screen in these hangout films would do the same. In life as in these films, by sharing music people reinforce their group identity, and bringing new musical expertise into the group like Bonnie and Dallas do is a way to express a desire to fit in. Music is equally important in other hangout films such as George Lucas's *American Graffiti* (1973), Richard Linklater's *Dazed and Confused* (1993), and Tarantino's own *Pulp Fiction* (1994), whether as diegetic music that we see the characters listening to and interacting with, or as extra-diegetic music that places the audience in the time or location of the film's setting. In a 2016 Toronto Film Festival blog post, "Ten Commandments of the Casual Hangout Movie," blogger Chandler Levack lists "Thou must have a killer, iconic, eclectic soundtrack" and "Thou must dance and sing along to a classic jam" as two of the commandments.[10] Levack and other critics see Richard Linklater as the primary hangout auteur, but Robert

Altman, Whit Stillman, and Tarantino are often cited as well. Only rarely are their progenitors like Hawks mentioned, and of these filmmakers only Tarantino is on the record as recognizing Hawks's influence on their own work. One could indeed posit Hawks as the primary instigator and developer of this genre. Such scenes of musical bonding are generally rare in Classical Hollywood films, and Hawks is the only director of this time who regularly makes a feature of them. In these scenes music is foregrounded as a social leveler and an important part of every-day life.

## Jazz in Academia: *Ball of Fire*

The two previous films focus on an outsider who integrates herself into a preexisting group by means of music. *Ball of Fire* (1941) is an intensification of this trope, as the outsider uses her music to fundamentally change the group that she joins. The music and language of the city streets combine to give a new lease on life to a group of eight staid professors writing an encyclopedia. Professor Bertram Potts (Gary Cooper) has been given the task of writing the article on "slang," and a conversation with a garbage man shows him that his research is hopelessly out of date. Potts resolves to leave his group's headquarters (the Totten Foundation, overseen by the dour Miss Totten, who is attracted to Potts) and do some fieldwork in the streets of New York. There he discovers not only modern slang but also modern music and, along with it, modern love. He hears nightclub performer Sugarpuss O'Shea (Barbara Stanwyck) singing with Gene Krupa's big band (playing itself) in a nightclub. Sugarpuss is on the run from her gangster boyfriend Joe Lilac (Dana Andrews), about whose illegal dealings she knows too much, and she sees in Potts and his Foundation an opportunity for an ideal hideout. Wheedling her way into staying at the Foundation, she quickly educates Potts and the other professors about the modern world. Sugarpuss finds herself falling in love with Potts in spite of herself, and Potts gets much more than merely a good encyclopedia article out of his experience.

Christopher Beach explores how language is used as a class marker in the film, and many of his findings apply equally well to music.[11] Potts's own stuffy academic language becomes influenced by slang as the film progresses, just as the film's classicizing score, which primarily represents Potts and his colleagues, is increasingly infiltrated by jazz. Alfred Newman's score foreshadows this highbrow/lowbrow synthesis from the very beginning. The opening credits are accompanied by a jazz-influenced romantic theme, a full string section and Romantic Hollywood harmonies in the style of Max Steiner mixed with a big band saxophone section. After the credits we see an establishing shot of Central Park, and the music immediately turns more "classical," flutes dominating instead of saxophones or wailing trombones, and settles into a jaunty scherzoso walking theme to accompany the professors' morning constitutional as they walk through the park in a carefully ordered formation (Figure 1.6). This group is thus established musically as highbrow and stuffy, albeit endearingly so. As the professors return home we hear a more subdued version of the theme accompanied by clockwork-sounding celesta, a subtle hint at the professors' well-ordered life, the effect of the music settling down with them into their day of research, which we can assume is just like yesterday's day of research and will be the same tomorrow. Their routine is soon foiled by the unwelcome entry of Miss Totten, the daughter of their patron, complaining about their lack of progress on the encyclopedia. Miss Totten has no musical profile: Hawks's heroines are musically and/or verbally talented, but like Miss Swallow in *Bringing Up Baby* (1938), Miss Totten is neither. Sugarpuss's musical skill and unique manner of speaking is bound to have a strong effect on this professorial ensemble. As soon as Miss Totten has departed a garbage man enters, hoping to get some help with a radio quiz question about Cleopatra. The scene establishes the professors as quite willing to engage with the public (that is, the film's wartime audience). Far from looking down on the lower-class garbage man, they are happy to help him and are intrigued by him. The scene is carefully written to appeal to the broad audience who might see the film: people "in the

*Figure 1.6* The professors' morning constitutional.
Source: *Ball of Fire.*

know" can laugh at the professors' ignorance of modern life, and those for whom the slang is new can still understand it from context, will sympathize with the professors' willingness to learn it, and will be happily brought into a knowledgeable "in" group. The professors' acceptance of slang as a natural part of language foreshadows their acceptance of jazz as a natural part of music.

The film's next music cue begins when Potts decides to leave the mansion for the streets. Through instrumentation, rhythm, and texture, Newman integrates jazz influences into the professors' "classy" theme in this bravura cue. A fugato begins in the strings, followed by the slow version of the theme (accompanied by "classical" violin arpeggios) as the professors bemusedly watch him depart. As Potts hitches a ride with the garbage man the full string section takes up the main theme at a quicker tempo, accompanied by jaunty flourishes in the winds that lend the music an especially light-hearted and optimistic tone. Potts's first encounter is with a newspaper salesman; he jots down some of the words the paperboy uses to shout out the news. When the paperboy notices Potts a solo alto saxophone takes up the theme's second phrase. This change in instrumentation is the first subtle taste of the changing style, the saxophone perhaps representing the way Potts hears these new words: he is starting to notice and understand them but is still trying to place them within his previous world view. The next statement of the phrase is introduced by trumpets playing a swing rhythm, and the theme itself is played with a light swing by a solo muted trumpet as Potts talks to the paperboy. The strings slowly fade out, replaced by saxophones, and by the time the next phrase begins the orchestration has transformed from string-dominated orchestra to big band. Potts is now on a crowded bus jotting down snippets of passengers' conversations. The Tchaikovskian wind flourishes of our first hearings of the theme are now replaced by big band licks. The playing becomes more heavily swung and gains in texture and volume in the next scene, where Potts tries to make sense of a baseball game. We have gone from the relatively quiet street on which the Totten Foundation sits to a busy avenue, then to a crowded bus, and finally to an even more crowded stadium, and the music has accordingly become louder and more extraverted ("hotter," in the parlance of the 1940s). Yet the musical material is fundamentally the same: Potts is still Potts, just allowing himself to experience a different context. Newman and the film editors carefully time these sequences so that we hear each statement of the theme in each new location. This continues in the theme's next repetition, now in full big band mode, when Potts finds some university students to listen to. The score breaks from the main theme and becomes low-down hot swing when Potts enters a pool hall, notating the colorful insults he hears the men hurling at each other. The score reaches a half cadence and is then cut off as the scene dissolves to Potts in the nightclub, where he is to have his fateful meeting with Sugarpuss to the exuberant tones of Gene Krupa's band's performance of "Drum Boogie."

Sugarpuss's performance of "Drum Boogie" will be analyzed in detail in Chapter 4 alongside the analogous scene in Hawks's 1948 remake of *Ball of Fire, A Song Is Born*. For now, suffice it to say that Sugarpuss's big band performance is the capper of Potts's exciting day, and it now becomes clear that, the score having foreshadowed the combination of classical and jazz styles, he and Sugarpuss will fall in love. This chapter is more concerned with Hawks's groups, so we will leave Potts and look at what happens when Sugarpuss encounters the group of other professors. The fateful evening of Sugarpuss's arrival at the Totten Foundation to hide out from Joe Lilac begins with the professors going to bed to the classical strain of their theme, delicately played by winds, strings, and celesta. It is interrupted suddenly by the rude sound of the doorbell. We hear Sugarpuss's romantic theme, last heard during the opening credits, played by the saxophone section as she enters the foyer. The celesta comes back in to accompany Professor Oddley (Richard Hayden) as he runs upstairs to hide from Sugarpuss, setting off the professors' theme again as Sugarpuss looks around the house. The professors' musical material alternates a few times with Sugarpuss's in this sequence, creating a stark dialectic between the two: the group (and Potts) is not yet fully prepared to let Sugarpuss into their lives far enough to change their own music.

This process of change begins in earnest the next day, with diegetic music rather than underscore, as Sugarpuss teaches the professors how to dance the conga. They try first to match the moves to a polka (similar in style to their theme), but in spite of their mathematical drawings of the moves on the floor they fail miserably and risk doing themselves physical harm. Sugarpuss demonstrates the right way to dance it, and the professors join her (Figure 1.7). Significantly, Sugarpuss opens a skylight before she demonstrates: she conditions the physical space with fresh light in the same way as she does with fresh music. One of the professors finally arrives with the appropriate conga record, much to the chagrin of Miss Bragg the housekeeper (Kathleen Howard) who, like Miss Totten, sees no propriety in these jazz-influenced goings-on. Potts leaves his class discussion on slang to discover all of the professors and Sugarpuss enjoying a conga line. There is no equivalent scene in *A Song Is Born*, which robs the remake of this important plot point of Sugarpuss (renamed Honey in the remake) changing not just Potts (Frisbee in *A Song Is Born*) but also the whole group of professors. This scene of musical bonding in *Ball of Fire* further motivates the professors' desire to rescue Sugarpuss from the gangsters. They help her not only because Potts is in love with her but also because she has had such a strong personal influence on them. In broadening their musical horizons, she has made them all better scholars, connected to life beyond their books.

The music in the rest of the film continues in the same synthesizing vein, moving rapidly between the professors' thematic material and the jazz theme.

*Figure 1.7* The professors attempt the conga.
Source: *Ball of Fire.*

Sugarpuss is occasionally accompanied by the professors' music, as when she talks to the group as they prepare to have Potts's bachelor dinner in the hotel: the first part of the cue is their theme, but it segues imperceptibly into Sugarpuss's, then back, as the conversation develops. Newman creates a musical space where both genres can coexist, implying that the relationship between Potts and Sugarpuss will also work out successfully. Potts realizes that Sugarpuss is truly betrothed to Joe Lilac and as he confronts her we hear her theme still in the violin but harmonized and orchestrated in a more "classical" manner: she has been influenced by Potts's sound world as much as he has been by hers. The next scene, when the group has returned to the safety of the Totten Foundation's walls, the difference between the styles is starkly displayed again as Miss Bragg the housekeeper accidentally sets off the phonograph, which the conga record is still on. She runs away with the machine as quickly as she can, then we hear a purely classicizing underscore that incorporates the professors' theme, "Gaudeamus Igitur," and "Genevieve" (which the professors sang together the previous evening). As soon as Oddley mentions Sugarpuss and finds what they think is the cheap ring Potts bought her, we hear Sugarpuss's theme again played by a muted trumpet; even at their most traditionally classical moment they cannot forget her influence on their group.

The final scene of the film ties the threads together, as the professors use their various fields of research to show how synthesis in love can indeed occur (mathematical proofs, historical and literary examples, geography ["two rivers converging irresistibly"]). Finally, Potts proves it beyond a doubt by kissing Sugarpuss; the professors leave them to their privacy and a final jazz/ classical flourish brings the film to a close. The insular group of professors is forever changed for the good by the modern outside influence of Sugarpuss O'Shea. Bonnie, Dallas, and Sugarpuss all use their musical knowledge to gain entrance into, and ultimately to re-arrange and even improve, the groups they join.

## Notes

1  See Molly Haskell, *From Reverence to Rape: The Treatment of Women in the Movies*, 3rd ed. (Chicago: University of Chicago Press, 2016) on the Hawksian woman. Haskell says that Bonnie becomes "a sobbing stone around the collective neck of civil aviation," but her analysis of Bonnie as a negative example ignores the forthcoming pivotal musical moment where she gives up sobbing (210).
2  Chion claims in *Film: A Sound Art* (New York: Columbia University Press, 2009) that there "is no soundtrack" because there is no auditory frame for sounds the way there is for images (491). While this is usually true, Hawks here and elsewhere gives his audio-viewers the very strong impression that what they hear is indeed contained by what they can see.
3  Christopher Small coined the word "musicking" in his book of that title (Hanover: University Press of New England, 1998). He argues that music should be thought of as an active verb ("to music") rather than as a static noun.
4  Leland Poague, *Howard Hawks* (Boston: Twayne Publishers, 1982), 29.
5  Manny Farber wittily describes the scene thus: "Jean Arthur is being blithe, snapping her fingers (the first of the block-headed swingers) in time with some fairly authentic calypso dancers who are being unbelievably passionate at ten in the morning." Farber, "Howard Hawks," in *Farber on Film*, ed. Robert Polito (New York: Library of America, 2009), 657.
6  Poague, *Howard Hawks,* 39.
7  Chapter 3 will show how this dynamic plays out with male choruses in Hawks's work.
8  This is not really the place for a discursus on drunk singing, but drunkenness is another site where male musicality (broadly defined) seems to be permissible: men who would never sing in public while sober often eagerly do so while drunk. Perhaps this is an example of drunkenness allowing for a carnivalesque approach to musicking and its masculine affordances.
9  Waterbucket, "Quentin Tarantino about 'Rio Bravo' – 2007," *YouTube*, 2007, www.youtube.com/watch?v=KjX010pdIro.
10  Chandler Levack, "Ten Commandments of the Causal Hangout Movie." *MOTIF(F)* (blog). May 3, 2016. www.tiff.net/the-review/the-ten-commandments-of-the-casual-hangout-movie/. Accessed June 25, 2018.
11  Christopher Beach, "Is Class Necessary? Preston Sturges and Howard Hawks in the Early 1940s," in *Class, Language, and American Film Comedy* (Cambridge: Cambridge University Press, 2002).

# 2   Speaking a Duet

Hawks's films are notable for their frequent absence of bourgeois-conventional heterosexual love relationships. This is reflected musically in that in Hawks's world the cliched orchestral love theme accompanying a verbal duet between two protagonists, the classic musical marker of such relationships, usually does not have a place. As shown in the previous chapter with *Ball of Fire*, when there is a love theme it is used for reasons other than merely denoting romantic love. In the case of that film, it is a marker of the incorporation of Sugarpuss's musical style into that of the professors, signifying beyond the Sugarpuss/Potts couple. Andrew Britton sums up this attitude:

> The Hawksian world view renders redundant (indeed undesirable) the ideologically normative view of the couple as producer of children and agent of social reproduction. Equally, the image of the "democratic" couple, in its bourgeois acceptation, becomes problematic: if the bourgeois world is unacceptable per se, the prospect of "equality" within it is deprived of its status as an ideal.[1]

While a conventional musical love duet brings together different male and female voices through melodic and harmonic material (through the usual solo – solo – duo structure), Hawks's anti-romantic dialogues highlight the opposition of the voices of the participants as they overlap and argue, creating suspense as to whether the couple will ever come together and verbalizing their inequality. *Twentieth Century* (1934) and *His Girl Friday* (1940) stage a series of arguments between their protagonists Lili and Oscar, and Hildy and Walter; *To Have and Have Not* (1944) and *The Big Sleep* (1946) both enact love through off-kilter hard-boiled witty sparring between stars Humphrey Bogart and Lauren Bacall; *Rio Bravo* (1959) and *Hatari!* (1962) both feature the not-so-romantic prospect of an aging John Wayne outwitted by formidable female love interests. The love duet that almost appears in *Bringing Up Baby* (1938) is undermined by the presence of George the dog and Baby the leopard singing along, as the animals keep the humans from getting too sentimental. When Hawks does stage a conventional love plot between two attractive leading players, as in *Today We Live* (1933), *Barbary Coast* (1935), or *Red Line 7000* (1965), the results are among his least convincing work in terms of writing, directing, and acting alike.

## Duets of Re-Marriage: *His Girl Friday*

Even in his more serious films, Hawks's dialogue usually acts like comedy dialogue. Only in his least successful or least "Hawksian" films (like *Today We Live* [1933], *The Road to Glory* [1936], *Sergeant York* [1941], and *Land of the Pharaohs* [1955]) does the dialogue ever become stentorian and melodramatic. In his comedies, Hawks's treatment of dialogue is especially carnivalesque and raucous, at least until the final sequences of the films. In *Talkies, Road Movies, and Chick Flicks*, Heidi Wilkins discusses the female voice in screwball comedy.[2] The "fast-talking dames" (a phrase borrowed from an earlier book by Maria DiBattista on the subject) come on strong yet, Wilkins notes, "seem to 'lose' their verbal proficiency towards the end of the film."[3] This pattern is borne out by Hawks's comedies, especially *His Girl Friday*. Based on the hit Ben Hecht-Charles Macarthur play *The Front Page*, which had been successfully filmed in 1931, *His Girl Friday* famously switched the gender of the second lead: instead of merely being colleagues, newspapermen Walter and Hildy become a divorced couple. Hildy (Rosalind Russell), having left the newspaper after her divorce from Walter (Cary Grant), returns to share the news that she is planning to get married again, this time to Bruce (Ralph Bellamy). Bruce is the opposite of Walter: a dull, slow-talking insurance salesman and a complete contrast from the brash, speedy newspaper editor. Walter, never one to take "no" for an answer, seeks to sabotage the wedding and hook Hildy back into her job as a reporter and, by extension, his wife. Using the planned execution of convicted murderer Earl Williams to his advantage, Walter flatters Hildy into covering the story and she sets off to prove Williams' innocence. Along the way the farcical intrigue forces the two back together, and poor Bruce is left to return to Albany with his mother.

Hildy's voice does indeed become more dulcet and higher-pitched at the end of the film (as does Susan's in *Bringing Up Baby*) when she decides to reunite with Walter. Wilkins notes that Hildy's voice changes to a more traditionally "feminine" register of submission when she converses with Bruce and Earl, and she finally speaks in this mode to Walter at the end of the film when she breaks down in tears, pushed by his scheming to her breaking point.[4] But throughout most of the film's running time Hildy gives as good as she gets in her scenes with Walter, matching him with every verbal blow. On the film's restaurant scene, film scholar Sarah Kozloff notes that:

the two apparent antagonists speak in an identical rhythm, in identical cadences, singing perfect verbal duets – which reveal that the two are spiritually and truly one. Their minds click away at the same pace and in the same rhythm (as opposed to the slow Bruce), just as their words do.[5]

The "feminine" ending of the film cannot be denied as exemplifying a common trope, though – this breaking-down of voice back into a traditionally feminine mode is something that even very un-Hawks-like screwball comedies have in common. It is especially apparent in George Cukor's *The Philadelphia Story* (1940) and George Stevens' *Woman of the Year* (1942), where Katherine Hepburn, presented in both films initially as a strong, independent woman, is "brought down a peg" by the male protagonist. But these films are Hepburn post-"box office poison" phase, and as has been commented upon by Britton and others, many of these films end with the humiliation of her strong and brash characters.[6] Audiences get the transgressive Hepburn as well as the submissive one, with the films ending by favoring the "safer" submissive option.

In *Bringing Up Baby*, released in the first period of Hepburn's career, Hepburn's character Susan Vance does everything on her own terms; she never submits to David the way Tracy Lord or Tess Harding do to their men in the Cukor and Stevens films. The mediocre box-office performance of the film has been attributed to the fact that audiences were tiring of Hepburn's brash femininity.[7] In *Bringing Up Baby* Hepburn does sometimes employ a more feminine way of speaking, but here it seems more as a way to humor David's wounded masculinity rather than submit to him, more like the way Hildy speaks to the infantilized Bruce in *His Girl Friday*. It is as if Susan thinks that David wouldn't be able to handle a brash way of speaking at those points; it is about his weakness rather than hers. Wilkins notes that Susan goes in the opposite direction, becoming even more brash, when she takes on the "Swingin' Door Susie" persona in the jail when she and David have been arrested for their unusual behavior.[8] Wilkins makes too much of Susan's supposedly high-pitched voice; while it is true that Hepburn's voice is higher pitched than Rosalind Russell's (or Claudette Colbert's, or Lauren Bacall's, or Paula Prentiss'), it is not really the pitch that sets her apart so much as her bright projection. Where Russell raises the pitch of her voice to speak in a more typically "feminine" way, Hepburn projects less and uses greater pitch contour. In her 1940s films (especially *The Philadelphia Story* and *Woman of the Year*) Hepburn uses her voice in the more usual screwball comedy way, starting out bold and softening at the end.[9] This is all evidence of the use of voice as performance instrument: as with singing in Hawksian groups, using the voice in a particular way tells a character's interlocutors something important about the speaker.

Back in 1934, in *Twentieth Century*, Carole Lombard as actress Lily Garland does not play by these rules, using her voice in wildly varied performative ways (including "softly") to get what she wants instead of bowing to male authority. Throughout the film she gives as good as she gets with John Barrymore as tyrannical director Oscar Jaffe, who also makes use of the widest possible range of his vocal timbres. The two characters constantly try to out-perform one another, and Lily never submits vocally to Oscar. One thing that Wilkins does not discuss in her book is the role that sound recording technology played in early sound film and its relevance to early dialogue performances. The narrower capturable frequency range favored certain types of voices, especially those with "cut" like Hepburn's. By 1934 the technology allowed Hawks and his sound engineers to capture the wider range of sounds produced by Lombard and Barrymore and by *His Girl Friday* in 1940 the lower pitch of Rosalind Russell's voice was more faithfully recordable. Had Hawks made the film in 1930 the vocal acting might have needed to be very different. Historians of film sound focus on the earliest years of the talkies, but important developments that increased fidelity and permitted greater complexity in the soundscape continued to happen throughout the 1930s, a period mostly overlooked in histories of sound technology.[10] Hawks himself mentions dialogue recording technology in his 1972 interview with Peter Bogdanovich:

> One of the reasons that they didn't do it [overlapping dialogue] is the sound men had trouble: if you had two different timbres of voices, if you had John Wayne and a girl with a little thin voice, one would boom out and the other wouldn't be there and the man couldn't switch fast enough and you wouldn't want it to overlap because he'd still be in the same key as far as the volume was concerned.[11]

By using voices with similar timbres, this sound recording problem was mitigated, as with the absurdly theatrical mode in which both Lombard and Barrymore speak in *Twentieth Century* and the lower pitch range of Rosalind Russell's voice in *His Girl Friday*, which matches that of her male interlocutors.

Although it is a film with very little music, limited to the opening and end credits, *His Girl Friday* uses musical structures in its dialogue more consistently than any other Hawks film. Mast discusses much of this dialogue stylization in his chapter on the film.[12] While it is famous for the speed of its overlapping dialogue, the film represents one extreme of Hawks's dialogue speed: at the other end are the late westerns, which have slower dialogue to match their slower overall tempi. Interestingly, in his late recorded interviews Hawks speaks quite slowly, more like the characters in his westerns (especially John Wayne) than the heroes and heroines of his earlier comedies. In her extensive analysis of Hawks's early sound films, Lea Jacobs finds that *Twentieth Century* has only limited overlapping dialogue. In the earlier film, the scenes' dynamism comes more from the combination of "gesture, block-ing, and speech" than actual overlapping.[13] We can hear the uniqueness of Hawks's approach to stylized dialogue when comparing scenes in *His Girl Friday* to those in the 1940 Lux Radio Theatre broadcast version of the screenplay, with Claudette Colbert and Fred MacMurray playing Hildy and Walter. The first duet between Hildy and Walter is played fairly quickly on radio, but nowhere near the speed of Russell and Grant in the film. Colbert and MacMurray's voices are also more mellifluous than those of the actors in the film, and they use a more stage-like projection, perhaps partly due to the exigencies of radio technology.

The film's first duet, in which Hildy and Walter see each other again after a long separation, is carefully written and performed to give it a sense of flow not unlike that of a nineteenth-century Italian opera four-part *duetto*.[14] This operatic *solita forma* (standard form) gives the composer and the singers a chance to explore a variety of facets to their characters' relationship through the use of a series of musical movements that contrast in tempo and affect, and the Hildy/Walter duet does the same thing. It begins with an introductory section (*primo tempo*) that sets the scene with the initial confrontation, in which the two characters are re-introduced to each other and provide the exposition necessary for the audience to understand their background together. The primary theme of Walter's original proposal speech about being there for Hildy "anytime, anyplace, anywhere" is also introduced. Then the two characters settle in for the *cantabile*, in which they discuss their divorce and reminisce about their aborted honeymoon. This acts really as a sort of inverted *cantabile*, about the characters' parting rather than their coming together. In a standard Italian opera this would be the most lyrical section of the duet, but here the characters make fun of lyricism and focus on its absence in their own relationship. When Hildy starts trying to tell Walter that she is newly engaged, the tempo of the speech accelerates and reaches its first climax when Walter looks back to when he first hired Hildy for the news-paper (thinking the "better offer" she refers to is another reporting job, not another husband). They are interrupted by a phone call from editorial assist-ant Duffy, giving us a brief respite from the argument, akin to the *tempo di mezzo* in an opera scene, and preparing us for the even faster and more emo-tional *cabaletta* to come. In the *cabaletta* Hildy is finally able to convey her news about her engagement to Bruce. The section also features a *mini aria* (a *cadenza*, perhaps?) for Hildy as she paints a negative picture of the life of a journalist. The duet finally winds down as Walter decides to meet Bruce, who is waiting in the lobby, in person. The main topics of conversation in the *can-tabile* were to do with the past, while in the *cabaletta* the focus is on the future: the contrasting ideas for Hildy's future held by Walter and by Hildy herself.[15] From here, the operatic metaphor can easily continue through the rest of the film: after a transition comes a trio in the restaurant as Hildy,

Bruce, and Walter get to know each other, and then ensemble scenes with the team of reporters alternate with smaller forms: the quiet duet between Hildy and Earl Williams in the jail cell, an *aria* (with commentary) from Earl's friend Mollie Malloy, a *buffo* trio of the corrupt Mayor, the Sheriff, and the messenger Pettibone. Hawks and his screenwriters and actors continue throughout to play with overlapping dialogue of various vocal timbres.

| | |
|---|---|
| *Primo tempo* | Hildy sits down, remembers Walter's proposal |
| *Cantabile* | They discuss their divorce, honeymoon, and Hildy's hiring |
| *Tempo di mezzo* | Duffy interrupts on the phone |
| *Cabaletta* | Hildy says she is engaged, and argues against a life in journalism |

Mast notes in his discussion of *Bringing Up Baby* that "George [the dog] and the humans talk at cross purposes."[16] This is true of many of Hawks's characters, especially Hildy and Walter: dialogue, when it represents conflict, is often deprived of its semantic meaning by means of the speed at which it happens and the overlapping that obscures it. Words become utterances. Inevitably, though, agreement is found by the end of the films as the characters discover how to speak in harmony. By the end of *His Girl Friday*, it has been shown that quick-witted Hildy and slow, deliberate Bruce are vocally incompatible. She properly duets with Walter, who can equal her verbal *sprezzatura*. It is her failed attempt at "singing" with Bruce that brings Hildy to the realization that Walter, with whom she can easily share a duet, is the appropriate partner for her. Like Sugarpuss and Potts in *Ball of Fire*, or Bonnie and Geoff in *Only Angels Have Wings*, opposing couples come together when they learn to understand each other's music, the "music" in the screwball comedies being the sound of witty, quick dialogue.

## Bogart and Bacall

Howard Hawks was instrumental in introducing one of the most famous Hollywood couples to each other, as Lauren Bacall was his and his wife's discovery, molded into a movie star with *To Have and Have Not* (1944) and brought to further stardom in *The Big Sleep* (1946), in both of which she was paired with Humphrey Bogart. The transgressive verbal duetting of Bogart and Bacall in their two Hawks films contrasts with what Andrew Britton calls Bacall's "redundant" presence in the other two films in which they co-starred – Delmer Daves' *Dark Passage* (1947) and John Huston's *Key Largo* (1948) – Bacall, Britton says, could have been "replaced by half a dozen other actresses without seriously affecting meaning, mode or conception."[17] While Britton focuses on Hawks's socio-political standpoint (i.e. his lack thereof) in

*To Have and Have Not* versus the much more expressly political *Key Largo*, the careful use of dialogue between the two stars in the former film also sets it apart and further highlights the uniqueness of Hawks's approach.[18] Britton argues that:

> Hawks emphasizes the union's impermanence ("Maybe it's just for a day"): the partners will stay together as long as they are "having fun" – "fun", as in *Bringing Up Baby*, being clearly defined, through the actors' incomparable repartee, as sexual pleasure.[19]

This is equally true of *The Big Sleep*, and not true of the much more earnest *Dark Passage* and *Key Largo*.

A digression on *Key Largo* is worthwhile here to highlight how Hawks's approach stands apart from other directors' practices. Britton is perhaps too hard on *Key Largo*, which is an important anti-fascist statement warning against the continued presence of fascist ideas even in America after the defeat of the Axis powers. John Huston was less concerned with music than was Hawks, and the comparison is useful to make: both directors were interested in American masculinity, but Hawks takes a "fun" optimistic view while Huston is usually much more serious and pessimistic. Huston's films rarely include memorable musical performances, with the notable exception of *Key Largo*.[20] The film is set in the Florida Keys, at a hotel run by James Temple (Lionel Barrymore) and his widowed daughter-in-law Nora (Bacall). One of Nora's husband's army buddies, Frank McCloud, turns up to visit on the same day as gangster Johnny Rocco (Edward G. Robinson) and his gang, who are looking for a hideout, come to the hotel. With them is Rocco's moll, Gaye Dawn (Claire Trevor), an alcoholic. A hurricane blows through, cutting the hotel off from the rest of the island.

The film, based on a play by Maxwell Anderson, uses the gangster infiltration as a metaphor for fascism. Gaye (Claire Trevor) is forced to perform of "Moaning Low" in exchange for a drink in a musical manifestation of fascist processes: she is compelled to re-live her past as a torch singer, colored now by her descent into drunkenness and her dependence on the gangsters who have caused that descent. What would have been an acted version of sorrow in its original nightclub context in this scene becomes a performance of the character's own subjectivity (Figure 2.1). Huston intercuts Gaye's performance with reactions from the other characters, the gangsters who have brought her to this place looking on in contempt and the protagonists barely able to look at her. With Hawks, music is always fun even when it is serious: even though the characters in *To Have and Have Not* are under a great deal of pressure from Nazi sympathizers when Bacall sings "How Little We Know" at the end of the film, she still enjoys the performance. Also absent from *Key Largo* are the witty and hard-boiled quips Bogart and Bacall share in their

*Figure 2.1* Gaye Dawn sings her torch song.
Source: *Key Largo.*

Hawks films. Here, the relationship is much more emotionally fraught (Bogart playing the best friend of Bacall's character's dead husband) and the dialogue, by future screenwriter and director Richard Brooks (not a man known for comedy, to put it mildly), is more pointed toward the plot and maintains a consistently serious tone. *Key Largo* features *dialogue*, not *duetting*. There is neither a musical nor ludic sensibility shared between the protagonists here, nor in Daves' *Dark Passage*, a very serious and almost experimental film about a man wrongly accused of murder. Their scenes together, while dramatically effective, have none of the amusing sexual frisson to be found especially in *The Big Sleep.*[21]

*The Big Sleep* is famous for its confusing and elusive plot, yet the film is strongly anchored by its colorful performances, especially Humphrey Bogart's as private detective Philip Marlowe and Lauren Bacall's as femme fatale Vivian Rutledge.[22] In the Raymond Chandler novel upon which the film is based, Vivian is no more than a supporting character. Marlowe is firmly at the center, and all of the other characters rotate around him. The film's production team needed to boost Vivian's character to make her a stronger love interest for Marlowe, especially with the casting of Warner Bros.' new star

Lauren Bacall, used to such great advantage in *To Have and Have Not*, in the role. An early cut of the film released to military troops in the South Pacific in 1945 is quite different from the final release version; closer to the novel, Vivian's part is smaller and there is more explanation of the complex plot. When it became clear that Bacall was going to be a major star, and after she and Bogart married (raising her star power even further), new scenes were shot to take advantage of their chemistry, increasing Vivian's presence in the story but leading to the removal of some heavily plotted scenes that make sense of the narrative. The final version of the film is high on atmosphere but even shorter on sense than the pre-release version.

The verbal sparring of the two leads in a number of duets contrast subtly to the Walter/Hildy duets in *His Girl Friday*. In the earlier film, Walter and Hildy know each other of old and quickly fit back into each other's verbal cadences. In *The Big Sleep* we witness the two characters meet for the first time and get to know each other, so their dialogue is more focused on showing off their quick wit and their skills at flirtation. Walter and Hildy both talk a wild streak, which is one way we know they are meant for each other. Marlowe and Vivian are more deliberate and low-key in the way they converse. Interestingly, Max Steiner's score for *The Big Sleep* does not match this affect, being instead surprisingly jaunty and light-hearted for such an often dark film (that is, at least after the stentorian main title theme, which acts like a musical red herring). Marlowe's dotted-rhythm theme mirrors the character's quick thinking rather than the violent or darkly sexual situations in which he often finds himself. The highly romantic love theme also seems to play against what we actually see of Marlowe and Vivian; a positive interpretation of this would say that the theme reflects the subconscious romanticism underlying these two characters who are so hard boiled on the surface. Or, to take a less charitable angle, perhaps Steiner could not figure out how to score them in a way that reflected what we actually see of them. Compare Miklós Rózsa's score for *Double Indemnity*, which is heavy and dark throughout, although the verbal exchanges between Walter Neff and Phyllis Dietrichson (Fred MacMurray and Barbara Stanwyck) are similar to those of Marlowe and Vivian.

David Neumeyer sees Steiner's score as one of the weaknesses of the film, along with its confusing plot: Steiner, he argues, was not sure how to deal musically with the changing types of films that the studio was producing and the result was a score that only sometimes matches the film.[23] Tony Thomas reads the music more positively, saying that "the music punctuates the action as vividly as gunshots and cleverly comments on the characters, particularly with its jaunty theme for Marlowe."[24] For Timothy E. Scheurer, the score is in fact a typical example of detective film scoring, which he contrasts with Jerry Goldsmith's score for *Chinatown* (1974).[25] That such varied interpretations of the score exist is an indication that the score and the film are not quite one. Peter Larsen provides a detailed analysis of the score in *Film Music*, in which he argues that the score serves to tie the confusing film together, helping the audience make sense of the interconnected scenes, an ideal example for him – because of the film's complexity – of how music plays this connecting role in classical Hollywood cinema more widely.[26] For Larsen, Steiner's score for *The Big Sleep* is one of the composer's best, disproving the frequent criticism of the composer's music that it is schematic, "a series of signal effects, simple musical comments on the action of the film."[27] Instead, Larsen claims, the music actually shapes the film, giving it narrative impetus and cohesion. Whether we value Steiner's score or not, he frequently puts Marlowe's theme and the romance theme (which we could hear as representing Vivian) in dialogue with each other, musicalizing and sentimentalizing the characters' verbal duets.

Marlowe and Vivian share a number of duets over the course of the film. Marlowe has been hired by Vivian's father, General Sternwood, to resolve gambling debts owed by his other daughter, Carmen. Layers of intrigue involving both sisters and their diverse contacts in the underworld lead to Marlowe and Vivian falling for each other and ending up together, this love story having been significantly expanded for the film adaptation. Their first meeting is at General Sternwood's house, when Vivian stops Marlowe because she thinks he has been hired to find Sean Regan, Sternwood's protégé. In this conversation, Vivian uses silence as a means of communication. Marlowe asks her, "You wanted to see me?" Vivian does not respond, instead looking him square in the eye, then she finishes pouring her drink. She finally says, "So you're a private detective," answering Marlowe's question with a statement of her own. Some verbal sparring, with no overlaps (unlike in *His Girl Friday*) until the very end of the first section of dialogue, leads to their discussion of Sean Regan. Bogart's speech is notably narrow in pitch range, only rarely expanding beyond a minor third. Bacall's speech is similar, choosing only a narrow range in contrast to Hawks's comic heroines, who have a wider tessitura. This was a conscious direction from Hawks, who had Bacall speak in a lower register than her natural voice in *To Have and Have Not*. This subsequently became Bacall's vocal trademark.

Their next encounter, when Marlowe brings a doped-up Carmen back home, is brief and in much the same mode as their earlier conversation: Marlowe is starting to find out more about the Regan connection. Marlowe touches Vivian for the first time here, a motion punctuated by a clap of thunder, perhaps literally a *coup de foudre*, although one would not think at this time that the two could possibly fall in love, presented as they are as adversaries. This encounter does not exist in the pre-release version of the film. Its inclusion in the final cut obviously helps us to remember Vivian's presence and prepares us to see more of her. The next duet begins with Marlowe finding Vivian outside his office waiting for him.[28] The dialogue and action here is more playful than in the previous scenes, which display wit but within a more serious, hard-boiled context. For example, here there is a mini-drama with Vivian wanting to scratch her knee and then playing with her glove, followed by a playful telephone call to the District Attorney's office where the two enjoy annoying and confusing their interlocutor. Part of the fun here is imagining the confusion of the sergeant, only some of whose dialogue is understandable through the telephone, making this a duet *con pertichini* rather than a full-on trio.[29]

The most substantial scene added to the final release version is the following duet, in which Marlowe and Vivian obliquely discuss the case thus far in a bar. This duet replaces a scene from the original cut in which Marlowe and the District Attorney summarize the case, catching the audience up to what Marlowe has learned so far. The song playing in the bar as Vivian walks in is "I Guess I'll Have to Change My Plan," an ironic choice considering the change to the film necessitated by Bacall's new-found stardom. The scene adds nothing to the plot (and in fact further obscures it by virtue of having replaced the expository scene) but adds considerably to the "fun" of the film. As such, Hawks's fingerprints are all over it. The two characters pause much less here than in their first duet, not quite overlapping but speaking directly after each other. This serves to give a strong impression of their verbal dexterity and punning ability. The next song we hear in the background is "Between the Devil and the Deep Blue Sea," followed by "You Go to My Head," further subtle hints at the developing relationship. A transcription of the central portion of the duet shows the two characters at work.

VIVIAN:  Tell me, uh, what do you usually do when you're not working?
MARLOWE:  Oh, play the horses, fool around.
V:  No women?
M:  Oh I'm generally working on something most of the time.
V:  Could that be stretched to include me?
M:  Well I like you, I told you that before.
V:  I liked hearing you say it.
M:  Hm.
V:  But you didn't do much about it.
M:  Well neither did you.
V:  Well … speaking of horses, I like to play them myself. But I like to see them work out a little first. See if they're front runners or come from behind. Find out what their whole card is. What makes them run.
M:  Find out mine?
V:  I think so.
M:  Go ahead.
V:  I'd say you don't like to be rated, you like to get out in front. Open up a lead, take a little breather in the back stretch, and, then come home free.

M: You don't like to be rated yourself.

V: I haven't met anyone yet that could do it. Any suggestions?

M: Well, I can't tell till I've seen you over a distance of ground. You've got a touch of class, but, uh, I don't know how … how far you can go.

V: A lot depends on who's in the saddle. Go ahead, Marlowe. I like the way you work. In case you don't know it, you're doing all right.

M: There's one thing I can't figure out.

V: What makes me run?

M: Uh huh.

V: I'll give you a little hint. Sugar won't work. It's been tried.

M: What'd you try it on me for? Who told you to sugar me off this case? […]

Marlowe allows Vivian to take the lead and do most of the talking, also hesitating more in his speech (using discourse markers like "uh" and "well"). Vivian is more direct, her only "well" coming when she modulates the subject to horses. Both speak primarily in short sentences, allowing the few words and their innuendo to communicate rather than extensive use of discourse markers or body language. They remain seated facing each other during this entire sequence, and Hawks uses a very traditional shot-reverse shot pattern throughout (albeit with both characters always in frame), so that our focus is entirely on the words. The only real physical action comes in the middle of this segment, when Vivian takes out a cigarette and Marlowe lights it. Donald Sutton observes that cigarette rituals occur throughout Hawks's films.[30] That this action is done so nonchalantly and without any verbal indications (no "give me a light") goes alongside the dialogue as further evidence that the two characters are becoming deeply in tune with each other.

We next meet Vivian again shortly afterwards, singing at Eddie Mars's gambling hall, a sequence to be discussed in Chapter 4. The scene exists in both versions of the film, but in the final release is read rather differently because we have seen so much more of the couple: their glances at each other across the room are more meaningful. The two meet again as they leave the gambling house, and this is the first time we hear their love theme, which swells in a stereotypical Hollywood way as they kiss. But it is immediately undermined by greater dissonance in the music as the conversation turns to Vivian's possible role on the wrong side of the case. Hawks does not let the scene turn into a conventional love scene. This is the last of Marlowe and Vivian's duets, as their next scene together also involves Mona Mars (the scene was reshot with a different actress as Mona for the final cut). The suspense of the final scene precludes its role as a duet, even though this is where Marlowe and Vivian finally confess that they love each other. Steiner's suspenseful music, which incorporates fragments of the love theme, mirrors the confusion of the two characters: should they make this a love scene or a crime-solving scene? The film's final sequence features Marlowe and Vivian, but is centered on the crime until the very end where the love theme swells. "What's wrong with you?" Marlowe asks. "Nothing you can't fix," replies Vivian. But their final look is not one of passion so much as one of confusion, playing against the music. They will have to continue working together to truly get to the bottom of the case. Whether in comedy or mystery, Hawks's foregrounding of duetting dialogue allows "music" to be made beyond the music, the characters speaking their duets to demonstrate their compatibility.

## Notes

1 Andrew Britton, *Katharine Hepburn: Star as Feminist* (New York: Columbia University Press, 2003), 182.
2 Heidi Wilkins, *Talkies, Road Movies, and Chick Flicks* (Edinburgh: Edinburgh University Press, 2016).
3 Wilkins, 11. Wilkins refers here to David Shumway, "Screwball Comedies: Constructing Romance, Mystifying Marriage," *Cinema Journal* 30, no. 4: 7–23 (1991), another work that discusses the verbal style of screwball comedy. See also Maria DiBattista, *Fast-talking Dames* (New Haven: Yale University Press, 2001).
4 Wilkins, 26–27.
5 Sarah Kozloff, *Overhearing Film Dialogue* (Berkeley: University of California Press, 2000), 174.
6 Andrew Britton, *Katharine Hepburn: Star as Feminist* (New York: Columbia University Press, 2003).
7 Gerald Mast, ed., *Bringing Up Baby* (New Brunswick, NJ: Rutgers University Press, 1988). Frank Nugent in the *New York Times* called Hepburn's performance "breathless, senseless, and terribly, terribly fatiguing" (Mast, 265).
8 Wilkins, *Talkies*, 32.
9 Wilkins discusses *Adam's Rib* (1949) in these terms. *Woman of the Year* is perhaps more interesting in demonstrating the shift, though, as the film's original ending, where Tess did not submit to her husband Sam (Spencer Tracy), was changed after negative test screenings. See Claudia Roth Pierpont, "Katharine Hepburn: Woman of the Century," *Woman of the Year (1942)* (New York: Criterion Collection, no. 867, Blu-Ray, 2017).
10 One recent exception is Helen Hansen, *Hollywood Soundscapes: Film Sound Style, Craft and Production in the Classical Era* (London: Palgrave, 2017).
11 Peter Bogdanovich, "Hawks On Hawks," *His Girl Friday [1940]* (New York: Criterion Collection, no. 849, Blu-Ray, 2017). This is archival audio of a 1972 interview.
12 Gerald Mast, *Howard Hawks: Storyteller* (New York: Oxford University Press, 1982), 208–242.
13 Lea Jacobs, *Film Rhythm After Sound: Technology, Music, Performance* (Oakland: University of California Press, 2015).
14 On the Italian opera duet see Philip Gossett, *Divas and Scholars: Performing Italian Opera* (Chicago: University of Chicago Press, 2006) and Harold Powers, "'La solita forma' and 'The Uses of Convention,'" *Acta Musicologica* 59, no. 1 (1987): 65–90.
15 David Bordwell examines some of the camera movements in this scene in his blog post "My girl Friday, and his, and yours," Observations on Film Art (January 16, 2017). www.davidbordwell.net/blog/2017/01/16/my-girl-friday-and-his-and-yours/.

16 Mast, *Howard Hawks*, 150.

17 Britton, *Katharine Hepburn*, 185.

18 The two films do have in common the foregrounding of music as a mode of communication, but in *Key Largo* the music resides with Claire Trevor's character Gaye Dawn, not Bacall's, and acts as an outside reference to the character's past as a nightclub singer, instead of as a present marker of participation in the group.

19 Britton, *Katharine Hepburn*, 187.

20 Huston's one musical, *Annie* (1982) was unsuccessful commercially and aesthetically. While some of his films have memorable scores, such as *The Treasure of the Sierra Madre* (Max Steiner, 1948), *The Misfits* (Alex North, 1960), and *Freud* (Jerry Goldsmith, 1962), they tend not to be as integrated into the audiovisual narrative as strongly as Hawks's films' scores are.

21 Much of what can be said about *The Big Sleep* applies equally to *To Have and Have Not*, to be discussed in Chapter 5.

22 In spite of having viewed the film a few times and read the novel, the plot is still rather elusive to me. Most critics feel the same way, but are divided as to whether this matters or not.

23 David Neumeyer, "The Resonances of Wagnerian Opera and Nineteenth-Century Melodrama in the Film Scores of Max Steiner," In *Wagner and Cinema*, ed. Jeongwon Joe and Sander L. Gilman (Bloomington: Indiana University Press, 2010).

24 Tony Thomas, *Films of the 40s* (New York: Carol, 1990).

25 Timothy E. Scheurer, *Music and Mythmaking in Film* (Jefferson, NC: McFarland and Company, 2008).

26 Peter Larsen, *Film Music* (London: Reaktion, 2007), 98–122.

27 Larsen, 121.

28 The position of the scene was shifted to slightly earlier in the film in the final cut, perhaps to space Bacall's appearances more evenly throughout the film.

29 In Italian opera, *pertichini* refer to interjections from other characters who are not part of the main number.

30 Donald Sutton, "Rituals of Smoking in Hollywood's Golden Age: Hawks, Furthman and the Ethnographic History of Film," *Film & History* 29, no. 3–4 (1999): 70–85.

# 3  Singing a Chorus

Many of Hawks's films feature male choral singing, sometimes central to the plot (*The Dawn Patrol* [1930]), sometimes narratively peripheral but featuring in an important individual scene (*Tiger Shark* [1932], *The Big Sky* [1952]), and sometimes offscreen but forming an important part of the score (*Red River* [1948], *Land of the Pharaohs* [1955]). Only in the two choral scores are these men trained choral groups; in the films where men sing together diegetically, they form an untrained group that breaks into song more or less spontaneously. Whatever the context, these male choruses act as another means by which Hawks musically stages group communication.

## Organic Solidarity in *The Dawn Patrol* and *Red River*

Hawks's first sound film, *The Dawn Patrol*, features a number of choral scenes. Focusing on a group of World War I English aviators, the film narrates a series of happy and tragic events in the lives of the men. Throughout the film, group singing is an important marker of the organic solidarity of the group. Hawks's films offer important statements of the structures of what Emile Durkheim called organic solidarity, the formation of social groups within modern society that go beyond the merely economic ties (which Durkheim called mechanical solidarity) that developed in the pre-modern period to become more meaningful and multifaceted communities.[1] Singing is a strong marker of organic as opposed to mechanical solidarity because singing has no material value; its social and emotional capital, however, is very strong.[2] By singing together, *The Dawn Patrol*'s group of aviators create bonds among the group's members, while also relieving some of the tension they feel and providing comfort to each other. At two points in the film the men sing the popular war song "Stand to Your Glasses (Hurrah for the next man who dies)." The first performance is serious, when the men think about their mortality, and the second comic, when the men sing with a surprisingly friendly captured German soldier, the song acting effectively as a satyr-play to itself. Hawks's camera captures the formation of the group through the first performance of the song, which happens early in the film. Unlike in *Only Angels Have Wings*, where the mise-en-scène of the shots takes in the whole group as they form a halo around the soloist, in this first song in *The Dawn Patrol* the first shots are of individual men; only when they actually start to sing together do we see a group shot. The editing and mise-en-scène serve to physically stage the group as it is simultaneously staged on the soundtrack.

The other song that runs through the film is not sung, but rather played on a gramophone: "Poor Butterfly" (Raymond Hubbell and John Golden, 1916), established early on as protagonist Scott's (Douglas Fairbanks Jr.) favorite song, which he calls a "jolly good tune." Scott is obviously the metaphorical poor butterfly, as he will lose his beloved younger brother to the war later in the film. It is unusual that he should be so closely connected to the song's female character. Scott is the first in a long line of sensitive Hawksian men who are contrasted to a more conventionally masculine figure, in *The Dawn Patrol* fellow flier Courtney (Richard Barthelmess), a category later including Montgomery Clift in *Red River*, Dewey Martin in *The Big Sky* (1952), Ricky Nelson in *Rio Bravo* (1959), and James Caan in *El Dorado* (1966). Many of these young men are shown to be musical, either singing or at least being fans of music.[3] The vulnerable young men in *The Dawn Patrol* use singing and listening to music to make their difficult lives that hang by a thread more bearable.

Like so many other elements of *The Dawn Patrol*, this trope of male group singing in times of hardship continues in Hawks's subsequent films. *Red River*'s score prominently features a male chorus. The film tells the story of a difficult and dangerous cattle drive from Texas to Missouri and enacts the conflict between the conservative Tom Dunson (John Wayne) and young Matthew Garth (Montgomery Clift) as to how best to manage the drive. As with *The Big Sleep* (1946) and *The Big Sky* there is some confusion and debate about Hawks's true *Fassung letzter Hand* of this film, which has survived in two rather different cuts.[4] The differences are in large part musical, and pertain especially to the use of the chorus. After Gerald Mast's detailed discussion of the differences, they have become known as the "book version" and the "voice version," due to the different modalities of narration they employ.[5] The book version is the earlier and longer cut of the film (133 minutes), enacting narrative transitions by showing pages from a fictional book, *Tales of Early Texas*. The shorter voice version (127 minutes) replaces the book pages with offscreen narration by Walter Brennan in character as Nadine Groot, the cattle drive cook. A few short scenes were cut from the voice version, and, significantly, the musical score was altered: the earlier book version features much more choral singing on the soundtrack than the later voice version.

Hawks told Peter Bogdanovich that the voice version, which was the final generally released version, was his preferred one, but critics debate the relative merits of the two.[6] Bogdanovich is in generally in favor of the voice version, while Mast prefers the book version. The film's final scene, the climactic fight between Matt and Dunson, was choppily re-edited and unnecessarily shortened in the voice version, although most of the other changes do not have a detrimental effect on the film's narrative structure and logic.[7] The two versions do feel tonally very different, however, and a comparison of the two demonstrates the importance of music within the filmic text. Critics tend not to notice the musical differences, and if they do they only say that the book version's soundtrack makes it somehow more somber or dark. Giordano Guillem, the editor of the Wild Side Blu-ray release of the film, claims that the music of the voice version is more Hawksian because it is "less grand."[8] While most of Hawks's films up to *Red River* feature a restrained use of music (with the exception of *Sergeant York* [1941]), his subsequent films with scores by Dimitri Tiomkin do have grander music, especially *The Land of the Pharaohs*. *Red River* in its book version could be seen as representing the first of the films in Hawks's 1950s "epic" mode, while the voice version is better described as the last film of his more focused 1940s "character-driven" mode.[9] Mast values the book version above the voice version because of this epic quality, but also for its lyricism, as opposed to the voice version's more conversational tone. He explains that "the slow, languid pace of the Book Version's visual transitions seems the appropriate poetic rhythm for this tale of heroic human action in awesome visual spaces."[10]

The book version's use of the chorus also helps to lend it this epic tone, as the offscreen chorus had already become a signifier of the epic mode since at least Frank Capra's *Lost Horizon* (1937), also scored by Tiomkin. The combination of the conversational dialogue Hawks was known for with the epic score and visual language results in a uniquely hybrid film, in which stylized conversation and high lyricism are in constant dialogue with each other. This is where *Land of the Pharaohs* will be seen to fall short, using only the epic mode in its score, visual language, *and* dialogue (because Hawks did not know "how a Pharaoh talked"). The later film is missing the conversational aspect that makes the earlier film such an engaging example of Hawks's storytelling. Mast also compares *Red River* to *The Big Sleep*, two films that on the surface could not be more different; he likens the obscure narrative of *The Big Sleep* to the lyricism of *Red River*. Both films have the general strategy "to shift the emphasis away from the external incidents and toward the underlying psychological and emotional interactions beneath the incidental surfaces."[11] The *Red River* chorus is another strategy to psychologize and emotionalize the story, although the musical strategy in *The Big Sleep* is very different, as discussed in Chapter 2, with Max Steiner's score frequently using a lighter, almost irreverent mode; Tiomkin was not known for a musical sense of humor. The only sustained musicological investigation of the score, by Kathryn Kalinak, helpfully places the two main choral songs into their context as, in Corey Creekmur's terms, "cowboy choruses," which exemplify "the ability to bring to the surface traces of repressed psychic states and unexpressed emotions."[12] Kalinak does not, however, mention the revisions that were made to the score for the subsequent wide release.

Before comparing the two versions more closely, a brief overview of Tiomkin's score is in order, as the basic musical material is the same in both versions. The score is primarily motive-based, with a few stand-alone sequences, Tiomkin's standard mode of composition and indeed that of most epic scores of the period; Max Steiner and Miklós Rózsa worked in similar ways. The orchestrations were by Lucien Caillet and Paul Marquardt, and the choral arrangements were written and conducted by Jester Hairston, who had also done the famous choral arrangements for *Lost Horizon*.[13] Three themes, "Settle Down," "On to Missouri" (called thus on the cue sheet), and what I will call the "Love" theme (due to its connection with Dunson's lost beloved Fen) feature heavily in the score. The most familiar theme is "Settle Down," as Tiomkin subsequently used the same melody as the song "My Rifle, My Pony and Me" in *Rio Bravo*.[14] All three themes are heard in the opening sequence of the film, the first two together in the Main Title (the two are often combined throughout the film) and the third in "Dunson Heads South." Some folk material is also used in the score, especially snippets of Stephen Foster's "Oh Susannah" (the "banjo on my knee" phrase), "Bury Me Not on the Lone Prairie," "She'll Be Coming Round the Mountain," and "I Ride an Old Paint." The treatment of the latter in the cue "Missing Cowboy" is notably similar to Aaron Copland's version in his 1942 ballet *Rodeo*. There is a consistent "Indian" motive, typical of the music used to score American Indians at the time, and a short lyrical theme that returns frequently in various modal and rhythmic guises – its minor march version later becomes the menacing Dunson theme in a clever use of motivic transformation by Tiomkin. There are number of memorable "effect" cues in the film, especially the chromatic counterpoint study of "Suspense at Dawn" that leads to the departure of the cattle drive, the *moto perpetuo* "Stampede," and the tour de force Prokofiev-like Indian Attack "Fight for Life."

The effect of the musical differences between the two versions becomes immediately apparent in the first few minutes of the film, as the arrangement of the opening credits music is different right away and the narrative mode (visual or aural) is introduced right after the opening credits. The book version features the male chorus singing "Settle Down," while in the voice version the song is played by orchestra alone. The book version has the horns playing the dominant at the very start, but the voice version cuts straight onto the tonic. The orchestration sounds much the same, although neither version was recorded particularly well and the chorus's words in the book version are almost unintelligible. It is likely that the same orchestral recording was used for the voice version, with the separately recorded chorus simply removed from the cue and the music started slightly later to shave off a few seconds for the slightly different editing of the credits. The chorus continues humming over the quieter verse of the song in the book version, while we are given a scene-setting text to read (over the same mountain background as the rest of the credits), while in the voice version the orchestra continues alone while we see the *Early Tales of Texas* manuscript, the only time in the voice version that the book is shown. In the book version the song's verse continues, while in the voice version a motive from the first part of the verse is strung out. This material is heard in the book version as the *Early Tales of Texas* manuscript is seen (the voice version simply cutting nine seconds of music), with chorus humming. The effect is to immediately make the earlier book version more epic, in that more musicians can be heard, and more human, in that singing is foregrounded.

The music continues in exactly the same way in both versions over the first shot of the wagon train approaching, only with Brennan's voice super-imposed in the later version. The music is only off by about two seconds, not enough to make any obvious difference in terms of synchronization with action or dialogue as there is no Mickey-Mousing or recitative-like writing in this scene. But the music in the voice version stops shortly after the dialogue begins. In the book version, as soon as the leader of the wagon train tells Dunson that he is "walking right into Indian country" and warns him against leaving, the music shifts to Tiomkin's "Indian" thematic material. Dunson's motive, here played by lushly romantic strings, is heard as Dunson talks about starting his own herd, then segues into the love theme when we see Fen running up to Dunson. The two versions re-align during Dunson's conversation with Fen (with a slightly jerky splice to the music in the voice version). The absence of music for this first dialogue scene in the voice version makes it seem more intimate, more akin to a chamber drama like most of Hawks's other films up to this point, rather than an epic. A tiny statement of the Indian theme is heard when Dunson tells Fen that the hardships she would face traveling with him would be "too much for a woman," but then the music returns immediately to the lyrical theme. Both versions then add the chorus singing "ah" at the end of the scene (we hear the chorus here for the first time in the voice version), but in the book version the orchestra fades out at the very end of the cue, leaving the chorus singing a cappella for a few final bars. The effect of this textural fade is lost in the voice version, in which under-score continues as Brennan speaks; it was very rare at the time to have a voice-over unaccompanied. The editors of the book version chose to have music playing throughout until this point, six minutes into the film, while those of the voice version stopped the flow of music earlier. The versions come together with the "Indian" music heard when Groot and Dunson see the threatening fire in the distance.

The music Tiomkin uses to underscore the dialogue in this sequence is rather busy in its rapidly shifting texture and key center. Tiomkin seems to be working too hard with this fussy cue, so unlike the matter-of-factness of Hawks's visual style and that of his actors. Dunson and Fen are scored with exactly the type of cliched love music Hawks avoided in his previous films, where the dialogue would have precluded its use.

One of the only moments in which truly diegetic music features in the film is at the beginning of the pivotal scene in which Dunson signs the men up for his cattle drive. A cowboy is singing "Goodbye Old Paint" accompanied by an unseen guitar, harmonica and a jews harp. The song continues over the gambling scene in which Groot loses his false teeth to his Indian assistant Quo. There is a short shot of the musicians just before Dunson walks into the room; as soon as he enters the music stops – this man means business, and has no time for music. The song scene that appears 11 years later in *Rio Bravo* finds a pre-echo here: John Wayne does not participate in the music making. In *Red River*, though, he stops it cold, while in the later film he allows it to carry on and acts as a contented onlooker, rather like a non-musical parent enjoying the activities of his musical children. While Wayne is musical in neither film, the difference between his relationship with music highlights the difference between these two characters.

One could posit that the film's non-scored scenes nonetheless feature a kind of music: during the cattle drive there is a constant lowing of the cattle in the background, the sort of sound Michel Chion calls the "fundamental noise" of a film.[15] The humming of the male chorus that we frequently hear in the book version alludes to the lowing of the cattle on the drive, a humaniza-tion of this fundamental noise. The one major chorus scene that exists in both versions is the initial round-up, one of the most exhilarating sequences in the film. The sequence begins with a rumble in the low strings (again alluding to the onscreen cattle's lowing), with dissonant contrapuntal chromatic lines moving in unpredictable directions in the upper strings. The music gradually takes on more tonally vectored direction, settling on a pedal note that accompanies an upwards-ascending line. After Matthew says they are "all ready," a 360-degree panning shot takes in the entire herd of cattle and all the men, horses, and covered wagons that will participate in the drive. When the panning shot settles on Dunson the music finally settles on a major triad after a series of suspensions, the continuous musical motion creating an analogy with the camera movement. Dunson says "Take 'em to Missouri, Matt" as the first section of music closes. Matthew shouts "Yee-hah!," setting off a *timpani tremolo* and further upwards chromatic musical motion, and a series of whoops from the men. Hawks gives each man his own shot, with fast almost Eisensteinian cutting, the rapidity at which we see the alternating individual closeups creating a sense of the size of the larger group. The whoops and hollers act here as other musical instruments, void of independent semantic meaning but with very strong affective meaning. The sound, editing, and rising chromatic scale create tension, which is finally released when the chord resolves and the offscreen chorus beings singing "On to Missouri." The wild whoops are replaced by the harmonious chorus and the individual closeups are replaced by sweeping long shots of the full group and the surrounding landscape: the disparate group of inarticulate men is musically unified for the difficult cattle drive ahead.

After this sequence comes a campfire scene in which the difference between the film's two versions is again very telling. The book version features the male chorus singing an arrangement of "Settle Down" a cappella over the scene. The voice version has an arrangement for the guitar/harmonica/jews harp group from the earlier signing-up sequence. Groot's short off-screen narrative heard here in the voice version might have been seen as clashing with the offscreen voices of the chorus, so the instrumental arrangement allows Groot's voice, and then those of the characters on screen, to be the only voices we hear. The instrumental version does emphasize the musicality of the men, but so does the choral arrangement, albeit in a less physicalized way. The offscreen choral arrangement speaks more to the men's inner psychology: music is an expression of their soul, rather than merely an outward activity. The subsequent conversation between the younger men is unaccompanied in both versions.

In the scene before the stampede the howling of coyotes contrasts to the fundamental noise of the cattle lowing. This suspenseful loud "silence" makes the entry of the music all the more surprising, in spite of the fact that the stampede is to be expected due to the obvious foreshadowing in the dialogue. The book version includes a series of closeup shots of characters' reactions to the noise of the pots as Teeler disturbs them as he attempts to steal some sugar, a rather rare case in Hawks's work of expressionist filmmaking techniques, which rhymes with the series of excited shots at the beginning of the cattle drive. These shots help to increase the suspense prior to the explosion of the music, which therefore has a somewhat less vivid effect in the voice version. The final differences between the two versions' music are in the narrative transitions, covered sonically by Groot's narration in the voice version and by the chorus humming over insert shots of the pages of the book in the book version. These short choral transitions again reinforce the motif of masculine community building.

Suzanne Liandrat-Guigues writes that:

> if anything changes at the end of the film it is the implicit appearance of law through the organization of a group which historically is not yet a society, but which is beginning to develop the idea of a distinction between what is and is not permitted.[16]

The extensive choral singing that happens throughout the first version of the film is a foreshadowing of this creation of a society: musically, an ordered community is already portrayed. The voices of men come together in harmony that serves as a maker of society as a whole.[17] Significantly, Dunson participates neither in the spoken nor musical society of the film (remember the scene when his mere presence stops the on-screen music-making in its tracks). He remains an outsider apart from the new organic solidarity of this community.

For Mast, the book version is the more preferable of the two because of its more epic quality. The film has in fact been read in epic/mythical terms, finding its place within what we might call the "matter of Texas," akin to the "matter of France," "the matter of Troy," the "matter of Britain," etc., that is, the chivalric romances of Roland, Homeric mythology, and King Arthur, respectively. The American mythology of the West is made more epic in this film by the addition of the chorus. This will also be true of *Land of the Pharaohs*; although technically history and not myth, it stands very much within the 1950s "ancient epic" tradition, in which there is frequent slippage between myth, history, and religion. Robert B. Pippin explores *Red River* in the light of mythology and its connection to political philosophy.[18] His essay (founded on the book version of the film) explores *Red River*'s narrative engagement with the coming of law and order, focusing on Dunson's struggles to establish an ordered society but paradoxically creating disorder in his every attempt: "Tom's means of securing order and compliance in fact destroy the order they seek to produce."[19] The chorus, again, serves as a reminder of this desired order. Kirsten Day finds even more direct parallels between *Red River* and classical mythology, in Dunson and Matthew's odyssey across America and their trials on the way to Missouri.[20] A further parallel that Day does not mention can be found in the invocation to the muses to "sing" at the beginning of the mythological epics and the singing of the chorus at the beginning of the book version of the film. The Classical rhapsode is another analog that could be explored: as in Homer and Virgil, Hawks's western characters sing to each other to recount stories of past exploits and solidify their communities.

Mast states that "the action will chronicle the conquest of these vast spaces, of human beings asserting their power and determination over those spaces."[21] The human voices of the chorus also dominate the image when superimposed upon it, as the humans dominate the land itself. For Mast, the key to the film is the contrast between Dunson as "builder" of society and Matthew as "binder" of society.[22] Dunson/Wayne's hardness is required to build a modern agrarian/industrial society out of the wild, untamed West, but Matthew/Clift's softness is required to keep it together, with compassion and rule of law. The superimposed voices of the chorus also serve as a societal binder: the men sing in soft, beautiful harmony, while dissonance is relegated to the orchestra. The chorus does not participate in scenes like the stampede or the Indian attack, being reserved only for scenes like the roundup in which we see men working together harmoniously, or for transitions that narrativize the events from the perspective of the present. The chorus foreshadows and dramatizes the Durkheimian transition from mechanical (Dunson the builder) to organic (Matthew the binder) solidarity, envoicing the organic solidarity that will have emerged by the film's conclusion. Most of this orchestra/chorus contrast is lost in the voice version, but in the book version it serves with great effect to re-articulate the main themes of the film.

## The Voices of the Oppressed: *Land of the Pharaohs*

The chorus in *Land of the Pharaohs*, while similar in texture to that of *Red River*, has a very different thematic role. Where in the former film the chorus represents the freedom of the cowboys as they form a new society, in the latter the chorus represents the voices of the oppressed. The film tells the story of the Pharaoh Khufu, who sets out to build a pyramid that cannot be broken into, so that he will not be disturbed in the afterlife. He forces his slaves to construct the pyramid, a monumental job that takes many years. The film has a typical "saturation" score of this period: the majority of the film is scored, often by a large ensemble playing at a loud dynamic level. According to McCarthy, Tiomkin's score, recorded in Rome, was the most expensive film score up to that time.[23] The score is an excellent example of the use of mid-century orientalist tropes, harking back in Hawks's oeuvre to *Fazil* (1928), although without the earlier film's contrasting use of European salon music. Stephen Meyer discusses this mid-century style in *Epic Sound*, which focuses on biblical epics, although the scores for other films set in the ancient world used similar techniques.[24] The style could be characterized as a mix between the sensual chromatic style of the bacchanale from Saint-Saëns's *Samson et Dalila* and Strauss's *Salome* with the march-like textures and dissonant harmonies of Prokofiev and Shostakovich and the film scoring language that Steiner and Korngold had developed in the 1930s. Like *Red River*, the film features a number of choral set pieces, although in *Land of the Pharaohs* the singing is linked more obviously to singers on the screen (even though we rarely see anyone actually singing). Unlike the earlier film, the singing here is, broadly speaking, diegetic: the characters even remark upon it, noting how the voices of the subjects and slaves modulate depending on their mood. Vashtar the pyramid's architect notices that "the singing is different; this time they're not happy."

Hawks said that he was intrigued by the power of the Pharaoh, who was able to "get the whole country to build his pyramid."[25] The subjects and slaves who build the pyramid are controlled by acousmêtres (the voices of the gods) and Pharaoh, the live god.[26] The funeral scene of the former Pharaoh is the film's first major choral set piece: the architect Vashtar comments on the slaves' happiness at moving on to the next life, expressed through their singing. The singing changes to the minor mode for the cowards, who will have no afterlife. The next choral sequence is the gathering of the workers, who have been promised an afterlife in recompense for their work on the new pyramid. Interestingly, the sequence of the building of the pyramid begins with a 360-degree circular pan, similar to the one just before the cattle drive begins in *Red River*. The Pharaoh's advisor Hamar, who narrates the film, explains of the workers that "their joy gave them song," but then "in the place of song came the drum." The 360-degree shot shows us how the music, whatever its mood, binds the oppressed community together.

Bogdanovich, in his DVD audio commentary, mentions that Hawks used music wall to wall in the film because he was insecure with the film's pacing.[27] Tiomkin was not concerned with notions of authenticity the way Miklós Rósza was, instead focusing on volume and aural spectacle. Rósza would have had an instrument that sounds like the reed instrument looks in the snake charming scene, when conspirators are planning the murder of Pharaoh's wife. Like many of Tiomkin's films of the period (including *Red River* and *Rio Bravo*) the score makes frequent use of a theme song, first heard sung in Arabic over the opening credits. But aside from standard orientalizing musical tropes the song has little deep connection to the film's setting or mood. In spite of its near-constant playing, these features make the effect of the music disconnected to what is seen on screen.

There is no choral music in the central part of the film, as the focus turns to the Pharaoh's and Vashtar's respective inner circles. The underscore continues unabated throughout, but the chorus does not return until the Pharaoh's death, mourning at his funeral. The chorus in this film is reserved for scenes in which the wider community is envoiced. Unlike *Red River*, which at its root is about community, *Land of the Pharaohs* primarily concerns individuals, although those individuals exist neither in effective dialogue nor in effective music. In *Red River* the chorus on the soundtrack reminds us of this community focus throughout the entire film, while in *Land of the Pharaohs* they are used in a much less sophisticated way, as not much more than local color, undermining the very sense of community the film would claim to put on screen. The humming during the sealing of the pyramid – by far the film's most effective sequence (largely due to Alexandre Trauner's production design) – is like the voices of the stones themselves, as put in place by the slaves. The germaneness of the chorus here only highlights the less effective use of music in the rest of the film.

One more example of male group singing (this time onscreen) demonstrates the centrality of this trope to Hawks's storytelling. In *Monkey Business* (1952), *The Dawn Patrol*, and *Red River*'s group musicking to display organic solidarity is inverted when the regressed-to-youth Barnaby Fulton (Cary Grant) leads a group of neighborhood boys in a "war dance" to get ready to scalp his perceived love rival Hank Entwistle. Unlike the earlier examples, where singing is presented as a positive social force, and even as an antidote to violence, here it is shown as a celebration of libidinal violence itself. In Hawks's world music is not always a positive marker of society, although when it is not it is used parodistically as in *Monkey Business*. Overall, Hawks takes group music-making seriously even when it is "fun." *Red River* especially offers a vision of America underlined by harmonious choral music.

## Notes

1 Emile Durkheim, *The Division of Labour in Society*, trans. W.D. Halls. (New York: Free Press, 1984).
2 Singing in harmony is an even stronger marker of organic solidarity, as the division into vocal parts mirrors the division of labor that characterizes organic vs. mechanical solidarity.
3 "Poor Butterfly" also turns up twice in *Today We Live* (1933), also played in an army hangout; much as one would hope for a deliberate Hawksian intertextual reference, the song was probably added in postproduction. No one in the film makes any reference to it, unlike in *The Dawn Patrol* where the aviators frequently comment on the song as Scott's theme tune.
4 *Fassung letzter Hand* is a musicological term referring to the last version of a score that the composer left behind (literally "the hand's last version").
5 Gerald Mast, *Howard Hawks: Storyteller* (New York: Oxford University Press, 1982), 337–346.
6 Peter Bogdanovich, "Hawks and Bogdanovich," *Red River [1948]* (New York: Criterion Collection, no. 709, Blu-Ray, 2014). This program includes excerpts from an archival interview with Hawks.
7 The ending was edited to appease producer Howard Hughes, who thought it too similar to the ending of his film *The Outlaw* (1946), which he was editing at the same time. Hawks had been originally slated to direct *The Outlaw*, but was fired by Hughes; threatening a lawsuit unless the ending was changed was Hughes' way of having the last word on the matter (Todd McCarthy, *Howard Hawks: The Grey Fox of Hollywood* (New York: Grove Press). Bogdanovich says that the ideal version of *Red River* would be the voice version, plus the ending from the book version ("Bogdanovich on Red River," *Red River [1948]* [New York: Criterion Collection, no. 709, 2014]).
8 Giordano Guillem, "Autopsie d'un montage," *La Rivière Rouge [1948]* (Paris: Wildside, 2013).
9 One could place Hawks's output into a loose periodization, describing the 1930s as being in the "men doing things" mode, and the 1960s as combining and distilling the three modes he explored earlier in his career (men doing things, character focus, epic), as seems typical of "late style" as defined by Edward Said (*On Late Style* [New York: Pantheon Books, 2006]). *Only Angels Have Wings* is the primary transitional film from the 1930s to the 1940s mode, as *Rio Bravo* is for the 1950s to the 1960s.
10 Mast, *Howard Hawks*, 342–343.
11 Mast, 300. Both films also contain significant narrative gaps, *The Big Sleep* being generally confusing, and more so in the final release version where a mid-film plot catch-up scene was cut in favor of more Bogart-Bacall duets, and *Red River* planting plot points that never play out, such as the duel between Cherry Valance and Matthew Garth. See Todd Berliner, *Hollywood Aesthetic: Pleasure in American*

*Cinema* (New York: Oxford University Press, 2017) for a detailed discussion of *Red River*'s plot holes.

12 Kathryn Kalinak, "Scoring the West: Dimitri Tiomkin and Howard Hawks," in Ian Brookes, *Howard Hawks: New Perspectives* (London: British Film Institute, 2016), 160.

13 John Morgan, Liner notes for Dimitri Tiomkin, *Red River*, Moscow Symphony Orchestra and Chorus, conducted by William Stromberg (Naxos 8.557699, 2003). In "Scoring the West," Kalinak focuses on Hairston's work as the first black musician to cross the color line in Hollywood, and whose choruses (including *Red River*'s) were racially integrated. Of course, this is only *sonic* integration, as these choruses are not actually seen on film. But Hawks also displays *visual* racial integration in his other 1948 film, *A Song Is Born*, discussed in Chapter 4.

14 The Love theme is also very similar to the song "Quand je rêve" from *The Big Sky*; the opening motive is inverted in the later song, and the tempo, structure, and affect is much the same.

15 Chion defines "fundamental noise" as:

> the continuous and undifferentiated sound into which symbolically all the other sounds of the film can fall or dissolve; the sound into which everything in a given film tends to be reabsorbed and pacified; either by covering over all other sounds at a given moment or by revealing itself as the background noise we hear when all other noises fall silent or return to it.
>
> (Michel Chion, *Film, A Sound Art* [New York: Columbia University Press, 2009], 478)

16 Suzanne Liandrat-Guigues, *Red River* (London: British Film Institute, 2000), 12. Liandrat-Guigues' main contribution to criticism of the film is her reading of it within the broader mythology of the American West, and how that effects the film's wider place within the western genre. Unfortunately, she does not consider the two different versions of the film, assuming that the book version is the only version.

17 Compare another great choral score of the decade, *Bambi* (Frank Churchill and Edward H. Plumb, 1942), in which the chorus stands not for men but for nature, not only singing songs but also echoing vocally the wind, rain, and fire that shapes the natural landscape. *Lost Horizon*, the first major Hollywood choral score, is somewhat more ambiguous: the chorus is tied to the idealized community of Shangri-La, not our corrupt modern society.

18 Robert Pippin, *Hollywood Westerns and American Myth* (New Haven: Yale University Press, 2010).

19 Pippin, 41.

20 Kristen Day, *Cowboy Classics: The Roots of the American Western in the Epic Tradition* (Edinburgh: Edinburgh University Press, 2016).

21 Mast, *Howard Hawks*, 308.

22 Mast, 333.

23 Todd McCarthy, *Howard Hawks: The Grey Fox of Hollywood* (New York: Grove Press, 1997), 534.

24 Stephen Meyer, *Epic Sound: Music in Postwar Hollywood Biblical Films* (Bloomington: Indiana University Press, 2016).

25 Peter Bogdanovich, Audio commentary to *Land of the Pharaohs* (Los Angeles: Warner Archive Collection DVD, 2007).

26 Coined by Michel Chion (*Film, A Sound Art*, 466), acousmêtre refers to a character who is heard but not seen (i.e. an acousmatic being).

27 Bogdanovich, *Land of the Pharaohs*, 69:00.

# 4   Humming a Tune

While Hawks's musical style is most strongly characterized by his use of music that is directly integrated into his narratives, his films often foreground music *as* music, where the audience is meant to notice the music and have an extra-filmic engagement with it, as opposed to typical underscore which signifies as part of a unified filmic text. In these cases, music is present on top of the diegesis – we might call it extradiegetic or supradiegetic. The clearest examples of these types of engagement are where the music is meant to refer to its own life outside of the film itself. The music here interpellates the audience as *music*. It says, "this is what music *does*; this is what music *is*; this is how you *use* music." In a Hawks film musical performance is never just performance. Instead, performing is another way for characters to tell each other about themselves, albeit in a more direct, presentational way than when music is used in the manners discussed in the previous chapters. In *Fazil* (1928), *Gentlemen Prefer Blondes* (1953), *Ball of Fire* (1941), and *The Big Sleep* (1946), among other films, popular songs lie at the center of the communication between characters and also outwards toward the audience.

## Song-Plugging in Venice: *Fazil*

The idea of a film having a hit song is frequently seen as an invention of the 1950s (as described by Jeff Smith),[1] but it is in fact a mode of cross-media marketing that dates back to the very beginnings of film, finding its origin in the illustrated song slides that sometimes accompanied performances in nickelodeons and other early cinemas and vaudeville houses.[2] While it might seem paradoxical for a modern audience, many silent films foregrounded their music by making it clear through visual means what specific song is meant to be heard. Hawks's 1928 film *Fazil* exemplifies this mode of musical discourse. The film is the story of an Arab sheik, Fazil, who falls in love with a Parisian flapper, Fabienne, while on a trip to Venice. The lovers are accompanied by a gondolier's song, "Neapolitan Nights," throughout their romance. Having been released in 1928, the film has a synchronized musical score for the theaters that were wired for sound, but even the musical arrangers in still-silent theaters would have known that "Neapolitan Nights" was to be played, for a transparency of the sheet music is briefly superimposed above the first scene in which we hear the song being sung by a gondolier (Figure 4.1).[3] The musical notation is not seen for long enough for the audience to be able to sing along to the whole refrain, but it is quite clearly marked as sheet music for *this* song. The sheet music cover of the song itself was marketed as being related to the film: it is labeled as the "theme song of the William Fox picture *Fazil*" and has a drawing of leading actors Charles Farrell and Greta Nissen on the cover, with the gondolier in the background. It was published by the Sam Fox Publishing Company, which had a contract with Fox Films (no relation).[4] The song had somewhat of an afterlife lasting into the 1950s and was notably sung by Mario Lanza and as a duet by Gordon MacRae and Jo Stafford. Most of the sheet music covers under which the song was sold include a gondola somewhere on the illustration, a mistake typical of the time when sings of "Italianness" were often derived from a variety of actual locales with little care for geographical authenticity.

*Figure 4.1*　A gondolier sings "Neapolitan Nights."
Source: *Fazil.*

The song, with music by the well-known composer of early film music J.S. Zamecnik and words by Harry D. Kerr, is plugged interminably throughout the film's synchronized score. We first hear the song ten minutes into the film, as Fazil talks to his European friends in Venice. Fazil clearly hears the song coming from the canal, and goes out to the balcony to listen. He locks eyes with Fabienne, who is listening from a balcony on the other side of the canal. There is no attempt to tightly synchronize the song visually, and it is impossible to tell what the gondolier was actually singing on the set. The musical notation is seen during the repeat of the opening A section. The sheet music shows up on screen again during the ball scene where Fazil first meets Fabienne in person. We hear it here in a waltz arrangement, which we can imagine is being played by the onscreen orchestra. The notes are superimposed over a shot of the orchestra toward the end of the sequence. The gondolier returns after the ball to take the couple on a trip through the canals, and he continues to sing the song. If the song was not in our heads already, it certainly is by now, thoroughly connected to the love of Fazil and Fabienne but also to a broader perspective of love.[5] Perhaps if we go out and purchase the sheet music we too can woo an exotic sheik or a perky French flapper.

The film's synchronized score, credited to Roxy Rothafel and arranged by Erno Rapee, is of interest for its use of orientalist tropes, especially monophonic "Arabic" chanting, which provides the film a striking musical opening and which then alternates with the salon-style music typical of the period (including, of course, the Neapolitan song). Fox marketed the film (and others of the time) as being accompanied by a 110-piece orchestra, but the reality was probably a smaller ensemble of 24–30.[6]

This song/film corporate synergy goes back to the beginning of sound film, the most successful case being "Angela Mia" from 1928's *Street Angel*, also a Fox film, and "Wild Orchids" from the eponymous 1929 MGM film.[7] "Neapolitan Nights" was mildly successful, with an order of 25,000 copies after *Fazil*'s premiere at the Carthay Circle Theatre in Los Angeles.[8] While it is unlikely that Hawks had any influence over the specific song that appears in *Fazil*, the use of a preexisting song in the film is not so different from the familiar songs that appear in 1953's *Gentlemen Prefer Blondes* (those from the hit stage musical on which the film is based): in both films, the film is used to further the popularity of the music.

## Juxtadiegetic Music in *Gentlemen Prefer Blondes*

*Gentlemen Prefer Blondes* is a loose adaptation of the 1949 stage musical of the same name, which was itself a loose adaptation of Anita Loos's 1925 novel. Only three of the musical's songs (by Jule Styne and Leo Robin) were brought into the film: "A Little Girl from Little Rock," "Bye Bye Baby," and "Diamonds Are a Girl's Best Friend."[9] Two new songs were added, written by Hawks's erstwhile *To Have and Have Not* collaborator Hoagy Carmichael and lyricist Harold Adamson: "Ain't There Anyone Here for Love?" and "When Love Goes Wrong Nothing Goes Right." In spite of its five songs a number of factors could be highlighted to argue that the film is only barely, if at all, a musical. Only the two female leads do any substantial singing. Five songs are not very many for a musical of the 1950s when producers such as Rodgers and Hammerstein were advocating for more faithful film adaptations of stage properties. And, *pace* Jonathan Rosenbaum, who sees the songs as integral, were the songs removed the film's plot would be barely altered.[10] In the 1950s, the age of the "integrated" musical, this is quite striking, but would not look at all unusual had the film been made ten years earlier. The songs are so strongly foregrounded in the film's structure, though, that it would be perverse to think of it as anything other than a full-scale musical. The detachability of the songs, however, serves to mark them as "songs" set apart from the rest of the film. This is not the world of *Guys and Dolls* or *Oklahoma!* Lionel Newman's score also alludes to the songs frequently in the underscore, most notably during the shipboard scenes, where we hear them in diegetic-style band arrangements as if played by the ship's orchestra.

Song lyrics, especially in a repeated refrain, can interpellate us more strongly than spoken words alone. Some lyrics in *Gentlemen Prefer Blondes* become almost like proverbs to live by: "When love goes wrong, nothing goes right." "Diamonds are a girl's best friend." The film is like a tongue-in-cheek instruction manual for how to be a gold-digger. Lorelei Lee (Marilyn Monroe) and Dorothy Shaw (Jane Russell) leave for Paris on a cruise ship in order to look for rich men. Lorelei already has a boyfriend (Gus), although she is not above trying out better opportunities while she helps Dorothy look for her own man. Hawks said in various interviews that he meant to portray Dorothy and Lorelei as caricatures, and the directness of their songs helps reinforce this.[11] The film goes from displaying over-the-top femininity during the dialogue scenes to even *more* overdetermined femininity during the songs, an extreme example of music taking over when words are not enough. In this film, though, words *are* enough, and the music takes on an absurd, surreal quality. The song sequences were directed by their choreographer, Jack Cole; Hawks was allegedly not even on the set for most of them.[12] But this does not make them any less worthy of discussion here. They are part of this "Hawks" film as much as any other element that the director did not have direct control over, like the source material, set design, or editing.

Unusual for the time is the film's "cold open" on protagonists Lorelei and Dorothy singing "A Little Girl from Little Rock."[13] They appear in bright red nightclub costumes, but at first we only see the two women, not a nightclub audience. This makes it clear that the cinema audience doubles for an on-screen audience, the proscenium of the nightclub stage doubling the proscenium of the cinema screen: the women are singing to *us*. After a single refrain of the song, the music shifts to "Diamonds Are a Girl's Best Friend," sung by an offscreen chorus as the opening credits roll. The choice of these two songs would have been obvious, as they were the two breakout hits from the stage version, made famous by and identified with the 1949 stage Lorelei, Carol Channing, who was not given the opportunity to play the role in the film. The scene then shifts back to the nightclub as "Little Rock" continues. This time, however, we do see an audience on screen (including Gus, Lorelei's boyfriend, enraptured by the performance). This opening sequence shifts the film's audience from being monodirectional spectators of the two women's performance to being sutured-in spectators of a more regular film based on classical Hollywood shot-reverse shot techniques.[14] The opening shot's foregrounding of this performance as performance is almost Brechtian in its effect, an aesthetic mode otherwise foreign to Hawks. This is perhaps more a marker of Jack Cole's presentational dance style than of Hawks being experimental. In other examples of musical performance on screen, the cutting pattern brings the audience in (sutures them), but this short pre-credits scene is entirely presentational. Jean-Luc Godard might well have had it in mind when filming similar games of presentation in his "musical" *Une femme est une femme* (1961).

The musical structure of *Gentlemen Prefer Blondes* is radically different from that of most of Hawks's other films. The musical numbers do not advance the plot of the film or act as narrative nodes; rather, they reinforce the plot and parallel its narrative. In Christian Metz's words, the music is *juxtadiegetic*, running closely alongside the plot but not necessarily *of* the plot.[15] Jack Cole's sung and danced narrative plays alongside Hawks's spoken one, highlighting the same central concerns through music and movement instead of dialogue. The musical numbers represent the film and its central relationship (Lorelei and Dorothy) in microcosm, in a mode of self-reflective performativity that contrasts with the usual Hawksian realism of the rest of the film. The two women start together and self-sufficient ("Little Rock"), they are placed in the narrative context of the ship ("Bye Bye Baby"), they re-assemble in the Parisian context ("When Love Goes Wrong") and they finally end up together, again self-sufficient in spite of having found new husbands ("Little Rock" reprise). Each also has her own number with a group of mostly men, further reflecting on their characters and representing their goals ("Anyone Here for Love" for Dorothy; "Diamonds Are a Girl's Best Friend" for Lorelei). Metz says that any "song from the film" should be considered juxtadiegetic, and he uses this film's two Styne-Robin songs as specific examples:

> Even though these pieces are almost always attributed to one character, and even though their very execution may be motivated by the diegesis, they "detach" themselves from the story and attach themselves to the film, from which they become inseparable in popular memory.[16]

This notion of inseparableness is very applicable to these two songs: most audience members would relate them to the film rather than to the stage musical in which they originated. This is a common mode within 1950s musicals, as earlier songs like "Singin' in the Rain," heard in the eponymous 1952 film, and "Dancing in the Dark," heard in *The Band Wagon* (1953) are firmly attached to those two films, rather than their original dramatic contexts (*The Hollywood Review of 1929* and the 1931 Broadway review *The Band Wagon*, respectively). Metz's point relates to the various modes of enunciation of film texts. For Metz, this detachable juxtadiegetic music reinforces the enunciation of the primary filmic text, or story. While this holds for *Gentlemen Prefer Blondes* and *Hatari!* (to be discussed later), it does not for most of Hawks's other films, where we have seen that music is an integral part of the primary narrative text, a means of intradiegetic communication.

For Rosenbaum, "When Love Goes Wrong" is the least successful song in the film; that other critics rarely mention it is evidence that they generally find it uninteresting. It comes at a trouble spot for any musical, whether on stage or screen: musicals need a number at the top of the second act that re-introduces the main characters while simultaneously carrying the story forward into its next developments.[17] In *Gentlemen Prefer Blondes* the song comes as our two heroines are in Paris without a franc and in their despair they sing and dance with the denizens of a neighborhood cafe. The number is the most traditionally presentational in this film in which all of the numbers are presentational. "Little Rock" takes us through the curtains into the nightclub, "Bye Bye Baby" travels through the cruise ship's stateroom and deck, and "Anyone Here for Love" takes us through the ship's gymnasium. "When Love Goes Wrong" does not change location, and only rarely changes shooting angle. Shot mostly from straight ahead, it is the most proscenitized of the numbers. The number is not without charm, although it is not helped along by its banal lyrics.

In addition to juxtaposing and paralleling the narrative, the musical numbers also present the relative state of the two actresses' stardom in 1953. While Jane Russell's contract guaranteed top billing and they have three duets and a solo each, Lorelei/Monroe is subtly favored in the musical mise-en-scène as she is in the main narrative.[18] Already in 1953 it was clear that Monroe was to be a major star, Russell of a slightly lesser order. This favoring begins in the opening number discussed above, when Monroe is alone in the frame for her vocal solos, but Russell has to share her shots with Monroe. A shot-by-shot analysis demonstrates this how this plays out:[19]

1 Long shot of both. They pull aside the curtain, timed to the stinger that starts the music; the camera tracks back as they come forward during the introduction and the first eight bars of the song.

2 Medium shot during the next eight bars, the camera following the two laterally, pulling in to frame Monroe alone for her solo (eight bars).

3  Long shot as Russell comes back in to join at the end of the next eight bars. The camera travels back again with both of them on the song's bridge.

4  Medium shot of both, including for Russell's solo: she does not get her own shot like Monroe did. The camera floats slightly sideways to follow her.

5  Long shot of both for the coda.
   [Opening credits]

6  Medium shot of both (beginning with a slight tracking out).

7  Medium shot of Monroe over Russell's shoulder. Russell leaves the shot, and the camera re-centers on Monroe.

8  Medium shot cutaway to Gus, watching from the audience.

9  Closeup of Monroe, the camera moving in closer as she sings.

10  Medium long shot of both, the camera keeping them in the middle of the frame as they move around the stage.

11  Medium shot of both, the camera continuing to move with them.

12  Long shot of both. They approach the camera, putting them in medium shot, then the camera pulls back as they end the number.

In this opening number, Monroe gets two solo shots including a closeup; Russell must share all of her screen time here with Monroe, and even in her solo numbers ("Anyone Here for Love" and the "Diamonds" reprise) she is rarely in closeup.[20] Technically, Russell gets to do more singing in the film, as she has a brief reprise of "Diamonds" in the final courtroom scene (one solo more than Monroe), but she is there disguised as Lorelei; in addition to plugging the song again, the sequence explicitly reminds us of Monroe through her very absence. The juxtadiegetic songs of *Gentlemen Prefer Blondes* fall somewhere between song-plugging and a radical deconstruction of movie music. Hawks's other films in which music is foregrounded as music are less disruptive in their structures but continue to explore music's inherent performativity.

## Songs of Safari: *Hatari!*

Chapter 1 showed that *Hatari!* (1962) reworks tropes introduced in Hawks's previous films, especially in the scene in which the photographer Dallas echoes Bonnie in *Only Angels Have Wings*. *Hatari!* also reaches back to *Fazil* with its song-plugging, in this case the song being the "Baby Elephant Walk." Henry Mancini wrote his piece expressly as part of the film score, while "Neapolitan Nights" was a pre-existing song in the studio's catalog, but the result is similar: a song used at an important narrative juncture in the film causes it to stick in the audience's memory. The "Baby Elephant Walk" was a bona fide hit, during the short-lived period in the early 1960s when instrumental-only songs could become hits, and in fact it won a Grammy award for Best Instrumental Arrangement. The primary instrument heard is an electric calliope that Mancini found in Long Beach, plus an E-flat clarinet doubling the melody above.[21] The song clearly hit its mark, as it was frequently covered throughout the 60s (by Lawrence Welk, Bill Haley and His Comets, and Quincy Jones, among others), and Hal David later wrote lyrics which were recorded by Pat Boone in 1965.

The song is set apart from the rest of the score through its style and instrumentation, boogie-woogie blues played by big band plus novelty calliope instead of the score's modular African-influenced big band music featuring authentic African instruments (in addition to the unusual sonority of six bass flutes).[22] The film prominently features a second song, "Just for Tonight," which is often played in the bar frequented by the animal trappers, but the song did not hit like the "Baby Elephant Walk" did. The latter is featured in a stand-alone sequence when reporter Dallas takes the baby elephants she has befriended to the watering hole for a bath. The sequence and the musical style stand out from the rest of the film, unlike "Just for Tonight," which is a standard ballad acting primarily as background music during dialogue. Metz notes how "songs from the film" like these are "willfully replayed and scattered throughout the film as accompanying music, which helps us remember them while partially de-diegeticizing them, leaving them finally [...] in an unavowed mode of address half-contained within the story."[23] *Pace* Metz, the repetition throughout the film of "Just for Tonight" did not help it become any sort of a hit; instead, the one-off use of the contrasting "Baby Elephant Walk" (albeit alluded to later in the film during the climatic chase through the town), tied to its memorably amusing dramatic context, turned out to be the more marketable song.

Hawks and Mancini were purposefully trying something new in this film; Dimitri Tiomkin was originally meant to score it, but he was not interested in the African sound Hawks was after. Mancini says in his autobiography that he welcomed the opportunity to score a "big-scope film," which he had not done before. Hawks had brought a collection of instruments back from Africa, and gave Mancini free rein to use them.[24] Musically the most arresting sequence in the film is the opening, as we are thrust into a tense rhinoceros chase before the opening credits. Mancini carefully modulates the tempo of the music with the action, finally stopping the music when one of the team of animal trappers is gored by the rhino. The rhino's breathing seems to form part of the score. Repeated modular patterns, some played on the African instruments and including the animal's breaths, in quickening and increasingly overlapping combinations, lend the scene its suspenseful air. This is the first time in Hawks's work that such a modular score is used. The film really has three disparate scores: the African-influenced music of the animal capture scenes, the lounge music based on "Just for Tonight" for the base camp bar scenes, and the elephant music for scenes featuring them and Dallas (the bathing scene and the final chase).[25] This reflects the uncertain and conflicted identity of the Hollywood film score in the early 1960s, as producers and composers moved away from the symphonic scores of the earlier era but were unsure what to replace them with, whether coming from the avant-garde or the popular music spheres. It also reflects the perceived need to have a hit song in a film, a mode of composition at which Mancini was to become highly adept. The difference between the elephant style and the rest of the film also brackets the song off from the rest, creating an easily-detachable hit.

## Songs in *Ball of Fire* and *A Song Is Born*

The first of Hawks's two musicals, *A Song Is Born*, his 1948 remake of *Ball of Fire*, is rarely commented upon in the Hawks literature. Hawks himself spoke out frequently against the film, which he directed only because he owed producer Samuel Goldwyn a film to complete his contract. It is, indeed, a pale imitation of the earlier film, although it alters the plot to enable a musical by changing the professors of diverse fields to a group of musicologists writing an encyclopedia of music. Musicologists are familiar with the film as one of the few that features their profession (the other popular one, a much better film, is *What's Up Doc?* [1972] directed by Peter Bogdanovich as an homage to Hawks, specifically *Bringing Up Baby*).[26] *A Song Is Born* is a very curious film, in that in spite of being about music it feels rather less like a musical than *Gentlemen Prefer Blondes*, even though the later film has less music and, as discussed above, does not attempt to integrate its music into the plot. This is largely because the score of *A Song Is Born* is so diffuse: the jazz musicians who feature each play their own music, and the two songs written expressly for the film by Don Raye and Gene de Paul, "Daddy-O" and "A Song Is Born," are rather unmemorable. Unlike the songs from *Gentlemen Prefer Blondes*, *Hatari!*, and even *Fazil*, these failed hits have had no afterlife outside of the film. The blues "Daddy-O," which holds the place of "Drum Boogie" in *Ball of Fire*, is a pale echo of its predecessor. Virginia Mayo as nightclub singer Honey Swanson looks ill at ease, compared to Barbara Stanwyck who takes charge of the screen as soon as she enters; even as flamboyant a musician as Gene Krupa cannot upstage her. Mayo works with Page Cavanaugh's trio, which has a much cooler style than Krupa's band. Mayo's performance remains bland throughout the film, and seems especially wanting when Hawks recreates scenes from the earlier version.

The laid back "Daddy-O" serves to stall the film, coming as it does after we attend a fast and furious jam session with Lionel Hampton and Louis Armstrong, while "Drum Boogie" in *Ball of Fire* serves as an exciting cap to the sequence of Potts collecting slang terms, with Alfred Newman's clever score that slowly incorporates jazz elements into the professors' old-style motif. This is one of the few places in Hawks's oeuvre where pace and structure are misjudged. Sugarpuss's allure is so striking to Potts because it is so different, the climax of his day out. Poor Virginia Mayo hasn't a chance against Hamp and Satch, and "Daddy-O" must rank as one of the worst musical sequences in a Hawks film, alongside *Red Line 7000*'s (1965) embarrassing "Wildcat Jones."[27] Even in his use of the camera Hawks makes "Drum Boogie" considerably more interesting than "Daddy-O." This is because Professor Potts is more effectively focalized than Professor Frisbee (Danny Kaye), his equivalent in *A Song Is Born*. The "Drum Boogie" sequence, as a shot-by-shot analysis shows, captures Potts's excitement at coming across this new style of music, and accordingly encourages the audience to share his excitement. Frisbee never shares any shots with the musicians, so he seems detached from the performance; this subtly leads the audience to feel detached as well.

### *Ball of Fire*

1   Medium long shot of Potts seated. The camera tracks right from him across the nightclub, settling on Krupa's band, playing "Drum Boogie," in long shot.
2   Medium shot of curtain with Sugarpuss's hand emerging.
3   Long shot of curtain, out of which Sugarpuss springs, the camera tracking with her until she is centered with the band. She starts to sing.
4   Long shot of band and Sugarpuss, from audience perspective.
5   Medium shot of Potts in his seat, looking confused by the music and words he is hearing.
6   Insert of Potts writing "Drum Boogie."
7   =4
8   Long shot of Sugarpuss and band (similar to the final position of 3).
9   Medium long shot of piano solo with saxes in front.
10  Medium shot on Sugarpuss as she sings her line ("See the drummer stompin'").
11  Medium shot of Krupa's drum solo.
12  =9
13  Medium shot side angle of Sugarpuss ("the cat's a killer diller").
14  =6 Insert of Potts writing "killer diller."
15  =13 (Sugarpuss says, "come on, Krup!")
16  Closeup of Krupa.
17  =4 as tutti chorus starts.
18  –9, sax solos.
19  Medium shot of Sugarpuss listening to the band.
20  Long shot of band (horns); trumpet solos (Roy Eldridge prominent).
21  =19 ("Boogie")

22  =9 ("da da da")
23  =19 ("Boogie")
24  =20 ("da da da")
25  Angle on Krupa solo (a closer version of 20).
26  =20
27  =5, Potts listening, still unsure.
28  Long shot of Sugarpuss and the middle of the band as she sings the verse.
29  Closer on Sugarpuss ("just gently").
30  =4 as Sugarpuss ends the song.
31  =20 for coda.
32  =25 for Krupa's solo.
33  Medium shot of Sugarpuss from side angle (similar to 13).
34  Different close angle on Krupa.
35  =4 as the song finishes.
36  Closer on Sugarpuss for her bow
35  =4 as Sugarpuss runs offstage, the camera panning right with her.
36  Long shot of audience applauding.
37  Medium long shot side angle of Potts with his row of seats. He asks the waiter what "Boogie" means (as applause continues).[28]

We see a variety of angles on the band, with some rhyming shots at particular points and quick alternation between shots at the mid-point of the number. The focus is mostly on Sugarpuss. We have been following Potts through the previous sequence, so we do not really need to see many reaction shots of him – just enough to tell us where he is in the space and what his general reaction to the music is (that is, confusion).

### *A Song Is Born*

1   Establishing long shot of the nightclub.
2   Medium shot of jazz combo.
3   Medium shot of Honey at the curtain; she comes out.
4   Medium shot as camera tracks with Honey as she joins the combo; when she arrives she starts bouncing.
5   Closeup of Honey's foot tapping.
6   Medium shot of Frisbee looking confused.
7   Master long shot of Honey and combo, framed by the audience. She starts singing.
8   =6 Frisbee writes.
9   Medium shot closer on Honey.
10  Medium long side angle on Honey and combo as they sing.
11  Medium shot closer on Honey.

12  =7
13  Medium shot of Horn section.
14  Medium shot of Honey from the side, as she walks into the audience.
15  =6 Frisbee watches.
16  =9
17  =6
18  =11
19  =6 Honey sings "I'll teach you"; Frisbee points to himself wondering.
20  =11
21  =7
22  =6 Frisbee applauds.
23  =1 Honey leaves the stage.[29]

The average shot length of the analogous sequence in the later film is rather longer (8.22 vs. 5.95 seconds) and there is less variety of shot types (12) than in *Ball of Fire* (22). In the earlier film Hawks achieves the focalization through Potts with his bravura opening shot, which starts on Potts seated in the nightclub and tracks all the way through the space, ending on the band (Figure 4.2). There is nothing like this in *A Song Is Born*, where we only see

*Figure 4.2* Establishing shot of Krupa's band.
Source: *Ball of Fire.*

Frisbee from one head-on angle, and he never shares a shot with the musicians. Unlike the earlier version, the protagonist is not connected with the space in which he experiences the music, leading the audience, whose identification with Frisbee has been established, to also feel detached from the source of the music. The rapid shifting to different angles gives *Ball of Fire* greater energy, as does of course Krupa's hot boogie more than Cavanagh's cooler style. *Ball of Fire* makes the audience want to be part of the excitement, as the onscreen audience literally is in the next sequence, when Sugarpuss calls them down front to get a closer view of Krupa's matchbox boogie. *Ball of Fire* also displays a stronger sense of musical community than *A Song Is Born*, as Sugar is very much part of the band, interacting with its members more than Honey does with hers (Figures 4.3 and 4.4). Sugarpuss laughs and jokes with the band, sharing the performance with them, egging them on ("Come on, Krup!"), and moving aside during their solos. Honey does not move from her position in front of the trio and does not make eye contact with any of the other musicians. Hawks also shows much more of Krupa's band than Cavanaugh's: the latter's horn section appears only in one shot, while Krupa's is featured frequently. The shots of the musicians are also more imaginative in the earlier film, with Hawks showing both Krupa and Sugar-

*Figure 4.3* Sugarpuss sings.
Source: *Ball of Fire.*

*Figure 4.4* Honey sings.
Source: *A Song Is Born.*

puss from a variety of angles and perspectives. We can imagine Potts as sub-consciously seeing Krupa's band as similar to the band of professors of which he is part: his focus is on the strangeness and newness of the whole experi-ence. Frisbee is only interested in Honey, in the manner of a conventional meet cute (which Hawks when on form and *Ball of Fire*'s scenarist Billy Wilder always tried to avoid).

For Ian Brookes, the importance of *A Song Is Born* lies in its role in the history of African American representation on screen, specifically its fore-grounding of an interracial musical ensemble in the group scenes that take place in the professors' mansion.[30] Brookes notes that the response in the black press, unlike that in the white press, "was almost euphoric about what it saw as an iconoclastic film."[31] How, then, to reconcile this clear historical importance with the film's obvious shortcomings? This is also a film that, as Krin Gabbard has noted, writes slavery and racism out of the history of jazz even as it promotes the genre and claims to offer a historical view of it.[32] The question that concerns us here is, how does this portrayal of jazz influence the film's overall sonic style? Not much, really: the only sections of the film that are true to jazz practices at the time are juxtadiegetic, serving only as sonic background for Professor Frisbee's peregrinations, or as markers for "jazz," used as exemplars for Frisbee's research. The jazz scenes do, however, give the film its only elements of enthusiasm and excitement. The only moment when jazz is truly allowed to be a plot point is at the climax of the film, when a performance of "Flying Home" is so raucous that a drum falls off the mantelpiece and on to the gangster holding the cast hostage. But unlike Professor Potts in *Ball of Fire*, Professor Frisbee is not changed by the new music he has found: Frisbee continues to react to the music as a scientist, where Potts made an honest attempt to enjoy it. Even the final orchestral flourish on the End title card is in the classical Hollywood orchestral style (and is then followed by Tommy Dorsey's rendition of "Going Home"). *Ball of Fire* ends with a jazz-tinged flourish, and a final playout over the end credits in a slow swing style, more up-to-date in 1941 than Dorsey was in 1948. Alfred Newman's score for the earlier film more effectively integrates jazz than does Emil Newman's for the remake. In *A Song Is Born* jazz remains jazz (albeit filtered through the white Hollywood system), and the highbrow score remains highbrow. *Ball of Fire* breaks down the distinction. Which film is really the more musically progressive?

## Bacall Sings

The effective editing of the "Drum Boogie" sequence is followed in Hawks's output by similar scenes of musical performance in *To Have and Have Not* and *The Big Sleep*, both featuring Lauren Bacall. I will return to *To Have and Have Not* in Chapter 5, but it is worthwhile here to discuss the mise-en-scène of the film's climactic song scene, "How Little We Know," performed by Bacall, Hoagy Carmichael as bar pianist Cricket, and his band. This song is rather less dynamic than "Drum Boogie" in its cutting, but coming as it does at the end of the film, we already know the characters and can read into their looks and gestures: that is where the focus is here. By this point in the film, Marie (Bacall) and Frank Morgan (Humphrey Bogart) have fallen in love, as Morgan has also decided to come to the aid of the French Resistance in World War II Martinique.

1   Medium shot of Cricket, at the piano, who beckons to Marie to join as the band tunes their instruments.
2   Medium two-shot of Marie and Morgan ("go ahead, go to work"); she leaves the shot.
3   Medium shot closer on Cricket with the band. Marie comes in front, the camera pulls back slightly to get her in focus, then starts moving with her.
4   Medium long shot of Marie with the piano behind; the camera travels center with her as the song starts.

5   Medium shot of Morgan watching.
6   =4 The camera moves back as Marie steps forward.
7   =5
8   =end of 6, with Cricket and the band in softer focus in the background ("who can tell?").
9   =5 Morgan catches the question that was just thrown.
10  Closeup of Marie. The camera moves slightly with her; she turns around and moves back to the piano, now in mid shot.
11  =5 The song ends, Morgan applauds.
12  Long master shot of the band, with a lot of cafe guests around. All applaud.[33]

This song is actually a dialogue, as only two main shots are used: one stationary of Morgan and one tracking of Marie (plus the closeup of her, but as it ends in a zone very similar to the tracking shot one can consider it merely an intensification of that single shot). In this scene, the cinema audience is fully sutured into the characters' dialogue. Even though the two characters do not share a shot after Marie "goes to work," it is obvious through the shot-reverse pattern that they are directing their looks toward each other. That Marie also focuses on other patrons in the bar heightens her subtle exchanges with Morgan since they are nervous about being seen as an obvious couple. An especially lovely exchange happens on Marie's sung question "Who can tell?" thrown at Morgan, who catches it with a smile. This song, unlike those plugged in *Fazil* and *Hatari!*, the juxtadiegetic songs of *Gentlemen Prefer Blondes*, or the scenes of performance in *Ball of Fire* and *A Song Is Born*, plays a role as a narrative node in the film, a concept to be returned to in the next chapter.

Bacall sings again to Bogart in their next film together, *The Big Sleep*. Unlike their dialogue scenes in the film, which we have seen act as duets, this song, "And Her Tears Flowed Like Wine" by Joe Green and Stan Kenton, is, strictly speaking, incidental to the plot and serves as a juxtadiegetic moment of performance-as-performance. It is happening when Marlowe enters Eddie Mars's gambling house, and he only drops in on part of the song (the central part, of course); as in the rest of the film, we follow Marlowe in and out of the room, never witnessing events that he himself could not see. This song, however, is somewhat less performative than the others discussed earlier in this chapter, in that everybody in the room (other than Marlowe) seems to be participating, although Vivian is the lead singer. The risqué and violent words of the song (like "He socked her in the chopper, such a sweet sweet guy was he!") also give Vivian an opportunity to flirt with Marlowe. This scene of performance does not exist in the film's source material, Raymond Chandler's novel, where the music at the gambling house is provided by a Mexican band that no one listens to ("no one was dancing or intending to dance").[34] Having the singing going on gives the venue in the film a more attractive mood than it has in the novel, where the focus of the guests is only on drinking and gambling. In the film, the variety of conversations we can see going on in the background, the respectable-looking men and women, and the playful cigarette girls make it a more attractive, aspirational space where Vivian, portrayed more sympathetically in the film than in the novel, seems more at home.

According to Peter Larsen, Stan Kenton himself is playing the piano in the scene, and Larsen sees the song's inclusion as a primarily commercial attempt to sell a popular song, bracketed off from the rest of the film: "the action is broken off, the film becomes a *spectacle*, the main female character of the narrative steps outside her role and presents one of the most popular melodies of the time."[35] Larsen is not wrong that there was clearly a profit motive for the song's inclusion, nor that it is primarily juxtadiegetic, but he underestimates the power of the song within the plot and within the sign-making system of the film. It gives Marlowe a chance to see Vivian in a different context, it gives Bogart a chance to look admiringly at Bacall, and it gives the audience an intertextual reminder of the many song scenes in *To Have and Have Not*. David Thomson offers a more plot-based way to think about this single scene of musical performance in *The Big Sleep*: "Why is Vivian performing at the club? [...] My best answer is that this whole sequence is a performance meant to divert Marlowe's eye."[36] Thomson's use of the word "performance" with its negative connotation as a kind of inauthentic arrangement is key: even the accompanying audience could be in on the game, perhaps an elaborate setup by Eddie Mars to distract Marlowe (and the film's audience) from his investigation. But this would point away from Vivian/Bacall's playfulness – if the song is a performance, it remains within Hawks's spirit of "fun."

Through examining these song scenes we can see that Hawks never uses a song merely as a song: it always has some storytelling role to play. Hawks's hummable tunes further demonstrate his musicality. While they do not always play such a *direct* role in storytelling as his other ensembles, they allow for easy communication with the audience, letting them become a part of the film themselves, having "fun" alongside the characters.

## Notes

1  Jeff Smith, *Songs of Commerce: Marketing Popular Film Music* (New York: Columbia University Press, 1998).
2  See Rick Altman, *Silent Film Sound* (New York: Columbia University Press, 2004).
3  No one told the gondolier (or the film's writers) that he should be singing a song about Venice, not Naples.
4  J.S. Zamecnik and Harry D. Kerr, "Neapolitan Nights" (New York: Sam Fox Pub. Co., 1926).

5 This scene is followed by what must have been a very titillating dissolve at the time, to a shot of Fabienne in a bed that has obviously been shared with someone else; the camera cuts to Fazil standing by the window in his pajamas. We learn before long that some time has elapsed and the characters are now married: the dissolve was only a tease of illicitness.

6 Ross Melnick, *American Showman: Samuel "Roxy" Rothafel and the Birth of the Entertainment Industry, 1908–1935* (New York: Columbia University Press, 2012), 323–324. Melnick incorrectly refers to *Fazil* as a lost film (478n82).

7 Michael Slowik, *After the Silents: Hollywood Film Music in the Early Sound Era, 1926–1934* (New York: Columbia University Press, 2014), 48–52.

8 Melnick, *American Showman*, 487n82.

9 "You Say You Care" is also heard as underscore early in the film.

10 Jonathan Rosenbaum, "Gold Diggers of 1953: Howard Hawks's *Gentlemen Prefer Blondes*," in *Placing Movies: The Practice of Film Criticism* (Berkeley: University of California Press, 1995).

11 The film is naturally very popular among gender theorists. See, for example, Laura Mulvey, "*Gentlemen Prefer Blondes*: Anita Loos/Howard Hawks/Marilyn Monroe," and Ellen Wright, " 'A Travesty on Sex': Gender and Performance in *Gentlemen Prefer Blondes*," both in *Howard Hawks: American Artist*, ed. Jim Hillier and Peter Wollen (London: British Film Institute, 1996); Alexander Doty, "Everyone's Here for Love: Bisexuality and *Gentlemen Prefer Blondes*," in *Flaming Classics: Queering the Film Canon* (London: Routledge, 2000); and Lucie Arbuthnot and Gail Seneca, "Pre-Text and Text in *Gentlemen Prefer Blondes*," in *Hollywood Musicals: The Film Reader*, ed. Steven Cohan (London: Routledge, 2002).

12 Todd McCarthy, *Howard Hawks: The Grey Fox of Hollywood* (New York: Grove Press, 1997), 508.

13 In the stage musical, this number is Lorelei's solo climactic 11 o'clock number, all about her; the shift of the song from the end to the beginning, and its alteration from "just a little girl" to "just two little girls," tells in microcosm the difference between the stage and film versions. The stage version is centered on Lorelei, with Dorothy merely as support, while the film becomes what Rick Altman labels a dual-focus narrative albeit with two women in focus instead of a man and a woman. See Altman, *The American Musical* (Bloomington: Indiana University Press, 1987).

14 Rosenbaum (1995, 45) sees this shot of Gus (Tommy Noonan) as creating a dialectic between the dull man and the vibrant women.

15 Christian Metz, *Impersonal Enunciation, or the Place of Film*, trans. Cormac Deane (New York: Columbia University Press, 2016), 118.

16 Metz, 118.

17 For example, "The Farmer and the Cowman Should Be Friends" from *Oklahoma!* reminds us of the central conflicts in the community and sets the stage for the musical's denouement. *Gypsy* features "Together Wherever We Go" in this slot to establish the second act's central trio of Rose, Louise, and Herbie, also using the concept of togetherness ironically to foreshadow the trio's dissolution.

18 Monroe, under contract to Fox, only received $18,000 for her work on the film, while Russell, on loan from RKO, commanded $200,000 (McCarthy, 504).

19 A model of this style of analysis of Hawks's work can be found in Raymond Bellour's "The Obvious and the Code" (*Screen* 15, no. 4 [1974], 7–17), a shot-by-shot semiotic analysis of a sequence from *The Big Sleep*.

20 In "Anyone Here for Love" she famously shares the screen with the scantily-clad USA men's Olympic team, also en route to Paris.

21  Henry Mancini and Gene Lees, *Did They Mention the Music?* (New York: Cooper Square Press, 2001), 110.

22  John Caps, *Henry Mancini: Reinventing Film Music* (Urbana: University of Illinois Press, 2012), 88.

23  Metz, *Impersonal Enunciation*, 118.

24  Mancini and Lees, *Did They Mention the Music?*, 108.

25  One in-between moment is the cue "Your Father's Feathers," heard when the captured ostriches get loose. The style of the cue has elements of all three: a generally loungey vibe with the high wind sound of the elephant walk (flutes rather than the E-flat clarinet), and African percussion.

26  Three others are Hitchcock's 1938 *The Lady Vanishes*, in which Michael Redgrave plays an ethnomusicologist whose abilities at aural dictation play a major role in the plot, the 1967 Disney film *The Moon-Spinners*, which has an ethnomusicologist as a secondary character, and Maggie Greenwald's 1990 drama *Songcatcher*, about an ethnomusicologist collecting Appalachian folk music. The stage version of *Hairspray* (2002) ends with heroine Tracy Turnblad deciding to major in musicology at college, a line most unfortunately omitted from the 2007 film version.

27  When I show the preceding sequence to my jazz history students they visibly deflate when Mayo (dubbed by Jeri Sullivan) starts singing, although her provocative costume does hold attractions for certain members of the class.

28  In the film this sequence runs from 16:06 to 19:46 (3:40), with an average shot length of 5.95 seconds.

29  In the film this sequence runs from 24:07 to 27:16 (3:09), with an average shot length of 8.22.

30  Ian Brookes, "More than Just Dance Music: Hawks and Jazz in the 1940s," in Brookes, *Howard Hawks: New Perspectives* (London: British Film Institute, 2016).

31  Brookes, 180.

32  Krin Gabbard, *Jammin' at the Margins: Jazz and the American Cinema* (Chicago: University of Chicago Press, 1996), 120.

33  The sequence runs from 85:08 to 87:02 (1:56) with an average shot length of 9.67.

34  Raymond Chandler, "The Big Sleep," in *Raymond Chandler: Stories and Early Novels* (New York: Library of America, 1995), 692.

35  Peter Larsen, *Film Music* (London: Reaktion, 2007), 104.

36  David Thomson, *The Big Sleep* (London: British Film Institute, 1997), 46.

# 5  Barking a Quartet

It's my leopard and I have to get it, and to get it I have to sing.

Susan Vance, *Bringing Up Baby*

Hawks seems to have had a fondness for quartets, as groups of four actors appear frequently throughout this work. Often this is a central couple plus two friends or sidekicks: John Wayne and Montgomery Clift in *Red River* are supported by Walter Brennan and John Ireland; Wayne and Dean Martin are supported by Brennan and Ricky Nelson in *Rio Bravo*; Humphrey Bogart and Lauren Bacall have Brennan (clearly one of Hawks's favorite character actors) and Hoagy Carmichael. These quartets often share musical moments. Hawks's 1938 comedy *Bringing Up Baby* features an inter-species quartet (two humans, a dog, and a leopard) and uses music at important junctures in its plot. Similarly to *Only Angels Have Wings*, its central characters make music together to cement their relationship, without their fully realizing it at the time.

Cary Grant plays Dr. David Huxley, a paleontologist engaged to be married to his dour fellow scientist Alice Swallow. While playing golf, David runs into Susan Vance (Katharine Hepburn), a madcap society heiress who leads him on a chase through New York and the woods of Connecticut for her aunt Elizabeth's pet leopard. The leopard, Baby, is a fan of the song "I Can't Give You Anything but Love, Baby" (by Jimmy McHugh and Dorothy Fields).[1] Susan is surprised that Baby would like such an "old" song (1928), but after all the leopard comes from the jungles of Brazil and they might not be so up-to-date there. Aside from the film's opening credits, the first time the song is heard is when Susan demonstrates for David the charm it has over Baby (Figure 5.1). The leopard takes a shine to David, blissfully nuzzling his leg while the music plays (in the living room, because in spite of the frightened David's exhortations Susan explains that the music sounds better there than in a locked bathroom). Susan has by now also fallen in love with David.[2] The version of the song they play on the phonograph is purely instrumental,

*Figure 5.1* Baby listens to his favorite song.
Source: *Bringing Up Baby.*

subtly leaving a space for Susan and David to complete it with the lyrics later. The first time they attempt to do this is a failure: on the road to Connecticut Susan runs into a poultry truck and Baby starts to go after the spilled fowl. Susan and David grab onto his tail and try to sing to get him to stay in the car, but to no avail. The song is fragmented, and Baby runs away to eat the chickens, ducks, and swans. They sing again when they arrive at Susan's house in Connecticut, conversing disjointedly to the tune as they try to get Baby to go into a cage. Later, during the evening search for the escaped Baby, Susan tries singing to bid the leopard back. David claims that he can't sing, Susan countering that he "has a fine strong voice." "But not for singing," David replies.[3] Finally they manage to come together with both the words and the music, in harmony no less, when they find Baby on the roof of neighboring psychiatrist Dr. Lehman's house. David is just starting to realize he is falling for Susan, revealing his "fine strong voice" and an ability to harmonize extempore.

The first time David and Susan sing together, when they first arrive with Baby at Susan's house, they converse, move, and sing all at the same time; in the scene outside Dr. Lehman's, they stop their constant motion and enjoy the moment of music-making. The first cut of the film featured a lengthy scene just before this, in which Susan speaks to David with excruciating obvious-ness about her desire to kiss him, any action on her desire interrupted by the sound of Susan's Aunt Elizabeth's terrier George's barking.[4] The decision to delete the scene allows music, instead of words, to speak more strongly about the characters' growing attraction to each other. David finds his singing voice at the same time as he finds love, as the film momentarily takes on the nar-rative structure of a musical. This is the first (and only) time in the film that we hear the full chorus of the song, complete with its lyrics, as Susan makes sure to stay behind and finish the last phrase as David runs off to catch Baby.

Peter Swaab provides a detailed analysis of *Bringing Up Baby*, in which he describes how David and Susan provide each other the partner that the other is lacking.[5] At the beginning of the film, David is seen thinking alone, trying to complete his brontosaurus skeleton, while Susan plays golf without any partners. They both find music as part of their discovery, brought to them by the leopard who brings them together. Nothing in the film points to either character being especially musical prior to this juncture. This is in contrast to *Only Angels Have Wings*, where the two lovers are both seen as being musical before they make music together, and to *Ball of Fire* and *To Have and Have Not*, where the woman is musical and the man is not. Baby and George join the performance as well, ensuring simultaneously with its absurdity that the scene does not lapse into romantic sentimentality and that the madcap couple remains within its comic context. Like so many of Hawks's films, *Bringing Up Baby* features a group formed musically, here singing in four-voice inter-species counterpoint. The couple on its own is not enough – a pair needs to be supported by the community. David's dead brontosaurus must be replaced by live animals to help him on his path toward love. Fossils do not sing.

The music in *Only Angels Have Wings* served primarily to articulate the film's plot at an important nodal point and, as also in *Hatari!* and *Ball of Fire*, to demonstrate how an outsider becomes part of the group, but in *Bringing Up Baby* the plot is actually articulated by music, the song "I Can't Give You Anything But Love, Baby" serving as a marker of the developing relation-ship: first it is on the record and only the leopard truly "hears" it, then David and Susan sing to the leopard with their own words to get it into the garage, then finally they give a "performance" with the leopard, singing together in harmony: a diachronically musical narrative rather than using music syn-chronically only at certain points.

## "How Little We Know"

In *To Have and Have Not* (1944) the music also functions diachronically across the narrative of the film. The film is set in World War II Martinique, a Caribbean colony of France, just after the Nazis have taken control. Hum-phrey Bogart plays Frank Morgan, a fisherman who is slowly convinced to join the Free French. Like in *Only Angels Have Wings*, and indeed many of Hawks's films, the action centers around a bar. The bar's house pianist Cricket, played by singer/songwriter Hoagy Carmichael, develops his song "How Little We Know" while the relationship between Morgan and recent arrival Marie (Lauren Bacall) is simultaneously taking off.

The musicalization of *To Have and Have Not* seems to have been developed by Hawks and the actors on the set of the film. The shooting script indicates a few sketchily worked out points at which music comes into the drama, but the film as shot places the music in more interesting positions. Cricket and his band are seen in the film at many points throughout, which were not all indicated in the script. The first time we see Slim (Morgan's nickname for Marie – she calls him Steve) sing with Cricket, the screenplay merely says:

> Intimate group around piano, where Cricket is playing some nostalgic song. Marie, sitting at nearby table with Johnson [an American on a fishing vacation], is singing. They have just finished dinner, and it is evident Johnson is making a play for her. Morgan, dining with Gerard at a table across the room, is studying Marie.[6]

In the film, the scene becomes a miniature drama as Marie leaves Johnson's table, goes over to Cricket, and decides to join him in singing "Am I Blue?" much to the delight of the assembled group and, especially, Morgan.[7] Hawks expands the screenplay's description of a static situation into a 14-shot narrative sequence.

Even greater differences between the treatment of music in the screenplay and the finished film emerge later. Most of Carmichael's contributions are in fact lacking in the screenplay.[8] The entire scene where we first hear Cricket trying out his tune for "How Little We Know" was added during shooting, as was Morgan's whistling of the tune in the next scene. The film's version of the singing scene following the tense night rescue of a French Resistance fighter says in the screenplay only that Marie is "standing by the piano, listening to Cricket rehearse a number with orchestra."[9] The expansion this song performance provides a respite from the preceding excitement. Cricket's performance of "Hong Kong Blues," however, is indicated in the script, and its description as a "number" seems to indicate that it was intended to be more substantial than simply background music. This stand-alone sequence was probably seen as Carmichael's chance to show off. There is evidence on other shoots of Hawks writing more scenes for actors he liked to have around, and this is quite possibly what happened with Carmichael.[10] Finally, the full performance of "How Little We Know" is not indicated in the screenplay at all, which merely says that Marie is "doing card tricks for Cricket and the orchestra."[11] The relationship between the protagonists is cemented here, helped on

*Figure 5.2* Marie dances into her future.
Source: *To Have and Have Not.*

its way by Cricket and Morgan's friend Eddie (Walter Brennan). Cricket provides the vehicle – the song – that both accompanies and describes the relationship, and Eddie provides somewhat cockeyed moral support for Morgan as he works his way through his feelings for Marie.

Hawks clearly knew that he could use music to show what dialogue alone could not. As with *Only Angels Have Wings*, the relationship between the protagonists is shown by means of the woman's musical performance and the man's awed reaction to it, rather than through the cliched dialogue of melodrama. *To Have and Have Not* is nearly always discussed alongside Michael Curtiz's 1942 film *Casablanca*, another Bogart-starring colonial French Resistance story. It would be impossible to deny that the later film was not intended as an attempt to repeat the success of the former, but musically the two films are very different.[12] In his detailed history of *To Have and Have Not*'s very loose adaptation from Earnest Hemingway's eponymous 1937 novel and its production history, Bruce Kawin sees *Casablanca*'s "As Time Goes By" as "drenching" the film in emotional nostalgia and the Carmichael songs in *To Have and Have Not* commenting on the action "in a light manner."[13] But the differences are more telling than merely the amount of music or its mood. *Casablanca* has much more underscore, and Max Steiner's score frequently incorporates the song "As Time Goes By" to play into the nostalgia theme of the film. The song serves as a link to the past. In *To Have and Have Not* and Hawks's other films the songs are very much about the present and they are spontaneous: "How Little We Know" points not backward to an ideal time but rather marks the newly-forming relationship between Bogart/Steve and Bacall/Slim. The song is developed across the film from piano noodling to a full performance just as the relationship develops toward its playful dance-confirmation at the end of the film (Figure 5.2). In Wood's words, "in *To Have and Have Not* (and in all the great Hawks movies except *Red River*) the past exists only as something to be got over."[14] The developing song helps to give the film its forward-moving temporal vector. The quartet here, Morgan and Marie plus Cricket and Eddie, who, while not musical, plays an important role in binding the group together and who adds his jaunty movements to the concluding dance, illustrates a different path to political resistance than that shown in *Casablanca*. The past-oriented music in *Casablanca* points to an idealized pre-war past that the characters fight to try to restore, while *To Have and Have Not*'s forward-moving musical vector points to a vision of postwar community. Hawks's film therefore seems more optimistic than Curtiz's. *Casablanca*'s characters are doomed to remember the past "as time goes by," while those in *To Have and Have Not* acknowledge "how little we know" about the future, only guessing that it will be full of love.

## Musicalizing Masculinity Out West: *Rio Bravo*

We now come, finally, to the most-discussed (and most-maligned) song scene in Hawks's oeuvre, the one in the 1959 western *Rio Bravo*. In the film sheriff John T. Chance (John Wayne) has found his trio of deputies to help defeat Nathan Burdette's gang, which has been terrorizing the town: reformed drunkard Dude (Dean Martin), young gunslinger Colorado (Ricky Nelson), and old-timer Stumpy (Walter Brennan). In the song scene the four men relax with music in the jail as they await the inevitable return of the Burdette gang, singing two songs: Dimitri Tiomkin's "My Rifle, My Pony and Me" and the traditional song "Cindy." Most critics find the scene an unnecessary distraction from the narrative or a disingenuous attempt to give Martin and Nelson a chance to sing for their fans. The scene's major apologist is Robin Wood, who devotes a large part of his 2003 BFI monograph on the film to it.[15] He sees it as central to the film and primarily as being about the looks that the four characters share as it progresses, and how those looks cement them into a group. Mast recognizes the importance of the sequence for these same reasons ("of course the two songs relate to the men's *esprit* as a group, as a Hawks community, as songs do in so many Hawks films") but Dean Martin and Ricky Nelson ultimately destroy the film for him: "My difficulties with this elegant chamber western can be reduced to four words – Dean Martin, Ricky Nelson."[16] Few commentators note the obvious fact that Martin's song, "My Rifle, My Pony and Me," has the same tune as "Settle Down" from *Red River* (1948). Mast argues that "the very shift of this identical melody from epic chorale to casual pop tune seems Hawks's deliberate announcement of his fashioning a more casual, domesticated film out of his formerly epic materials."[17] While Mast makes a valid point, and *Rio Bravo* is certainly in Hawks's later chamber mode and is an exemplar of the "hangout" film, the song is more than a casual pop tune. On the surface it is understandable that it should be read this way and Paul Francis Webster's dull lyrics do not lend it any extra musical value, but its positioning straight after the film's other major music-centric scene, in which Dude decides not to drink any more upon hearing the "Degüello," played by Burdette's gang to worry our heroes, puts "Purple Light" in a very powerful dialectic position.[18] One might be reminded of Noël Coward's quip in *Private Lives*: "Extraordinary how potent cheap music is."

Robin Wood also searches out the scene's homoerotic subtext. He notes that Dude and Colorado barely speak to each other throughout the film, and that "their relationship (prior to the song sequence) is conducted entirely through 'the look,' and the looks are eloquent."[19] He demonstrates that these looks continue throughout the song. According to Wood, Dude's song is "decidedly masculine" and on the second verse "Colorado takes up the words, Dude whistling each phrase, like an echo, the two exchanging intimate looks: the solo has become something resembling a love duet."[20] Wood's argument stops short there, and therefore is not as convincing as it might have been. Had Wood known of Philip Brett's work on "musicality" as marker for homosexuality and, especially, his article on Schubert's piano duets, he could have added more nuance to the argument.[21] In this scene, the shared visual looks are similar to the physical overlapping of hands that Brett discusses in his work on Schubert. Of course any shared live music making will involve looking at the other musicians, but the positioning of Hawks's camera heightens the looks in this sequence: Hawks could have put the four musicians (three active, one [Wayne] passive) in group shots, but, as will be analyzed in detail below, instead he shows them looking at each other in individual shots. This also serves to suture the viewer into the process. We stand in for the looked-at partner. The performers here do not share a musical instrument, but they do share the vision-machine that is the cinema. They share the same flat space gazed upon by the audience. Such group performance in cinema can sometimes be more intense than it would be on a stage, if the director decides to make it so, as Hawks does, by using camera angles and editing to intensify the notion of shared space, looks, and sound.

The "Degüello" scene and the song scene sit in a multifaceted dialectical relationship with each other (music made by *them*: music made by *us*; tension:release; trumpet:voice; minor:major), and the scene itself features two songs that are in turn dialectically related to each other. In "My Rifle" Dude takes the lead; in "Cindy" Colorado takes the lead. The first song is languorous, the second enthusiastic. The first is composed by Tiomkin, the second is a folk song. The first is about a man, the second about a woman.

Film scholar David Arnold points out various musical similarities between *Rio Bravo* and Fred Zinnemann's *High Noon* (1952), also scored by Tiomkin, namely the use of both plot-driven and incidental music (although, as we have seen, this is not at all uncommon in Hawks).[22] Arnold also places the song scene into the tradition of singing cowboys, a valid, if obvious, point. Arnold is one of the many critics who takes issue with the scene:

> Martin's delivery is at least neutral, if characteristically smooth, but Nelson is either intent on foregrounding or incapable of stifling a specifically 50s pop-rockabilly simpering. The spectacle of his tarted-up cowboy guitar, which looks like it came from the Sears and Roebuck catalog, adds to the unsettling effect.[23]

The positioning of the song within the rockabilly genre is undeniable, heightened even further by the extra reverb added in the sound mixing of the song. Arnold does not fully understand Ricky Nelson's positioning in late-fifties pop music, however:

> "Cindy Cindy" is here delivered in the manner of a late-fifties long-haired Elvis wannabe. Watching this scene it's clear why Hawks has Nelson sitting on a table throughout: if he were allowed to get up on his hind legs he'd turn it into a whole different kind of show.[24]

Nelson did not have especially long hair, nor was he much of a hip-swinger or blues singer. He was, in fact, a model of American bourgeois domesticity, a safer (read: whiter) alternative to Elvis Presley. Having got his start on his parents' television program *The Adventures of Ozzie and Harriet* (1952–1966), he was perceived as the wholesome sort of teenager most parents would not mind their daughters bringing home. Also, he is sitting because this is a relaxed scene; if he stood up to sing it would make little dramatic sense. Although Nelson is no Montgomery Clift, his post-adolescent swagger fits the character and its narrative function very well. Nelson's next film, the 1960 World War II comedy *The Wackiest Ship in the Army*, shows how well he is used in *Rio Bravo* comparatively. In *The Wackiest Ship*, directed by Richard Murphy, Nelson plays an earnest young Ensign, second in command to Jack Lemmon. He is given an opportunity to sing early in film when he goes to the Officers' Club in Queensland, joining in to sing "Do You Know What It Means to Miss New Orleans" for no compelling reason and with reverb added like in *Rio Bravo*. In the later film the song is shoehorned in; while the same has been said of the songs in Hawks's film, the role the song scene has in the narrative, and Colorado/Nelson's role within the scene, shows how different Hawks was from a journeyman director like Murphy.[25] With Hawks, everything in the film contributes to the storytelling. Playing Colorado also gave Nelson the chance to play a character with some grit, which he did not have either on television in *The Adventures of Ozzie and Harriet* or in his next films. In *Rio Bravo* Nelson fits all of the late-fifties signifiers of the cocky but charming teenager, and serves as a complementary fourth in the film's central quartet.

Like the "closed forms" of the duets in *His Girl Friday*, the song scene shows similarity with the usual structure of Italian opera scenes: a slow section (*cantabile*) is followed by a fast section (*cabaletta*). A shot by shot analysis further demonstrates the careful structure of the scene.

1   Fade-in to medium shot of Dude, lying down, who begins singing (a *cappella*): "*The sun is sinking in the West. The cattle go down to the stream.*"
2   Medium long shot of Chance at the coffee (Dude sings: "*The redwing settles in her nest*"). Camera starts traveling left with Chance as he walks toward Dude.
3   Long shot as Chance enters the other room (Dude sings "*It's time for a cowboy to dream*"). Camera follows Chance left, discovering Colorado, then Dude and Stumpy. Dude sings "*Purple light in the canyon.*" Colorado starts playing his guitar and Stumpy starts playing his harmonica when we see them. Picture of all four in shot (Figure 5.3).

*Figure 5.3* Sheriff Chance and his deputies.
Source: *Rio Bravo.*

4   Medium shot of Dude (closer than 1): *"That's where I long to be with my three good companions, just my rifle, pony and me."*

5   Medium shot of Colorado *"Gonna hang my"*

6   Medium shot of Stumpy *"sombrero on the limb of a"*

7   Medium shot of Chance smiling on *"tree. Comin' home"*

8   =4 *"sweetheart darlin', just my rifle, pony and me."* Dude gestures to Colorado.

9   =5 Colorado sings: *"Whippoorwill* [Dude whistles, Colorado smiles at him; the best little moment of the sequence] *in the willow"*

10  =4 Dude [Dude whistles]

11  =5 Colorado: *"sings a sweet* [whistle] *melody"*

12  =4 Dude starts humming into *"Ridin' to"*

13  =5 Colorado: *"ridin' to"*

14  =4 Dude *"Amarillo"* (quick look to Colorado)

15  =5 Colorado: *"Amarillo,"*

16  =4 Dude: *"just my rifle, pony and me."*

17  =5 Colorado: *"No more cows"*

18  =4 Dude: *"no more cows"*

19  =5 Colorado: *"to be ropin',"* Dude offscreen: *"to be ropin',"* Colorado: *"no more strays"*

20  =6 Stumpy listening. Dude: *"no more strays"* Colorado: *"will I see"* Dude overlaps: *"Round the bend"* Colorado: *"round the bend"*

21  Medium long shot of trio. Dude: *"she'll be waitin' "* Colorado: *"she'll be waitin' "* Both: *"for my rifle, pony and me, for my rifle, my pony and me."* Dialogue. Stumpy: *"Say, that's real pretty. Go on, play some more. Why don't you play something I can sing with you?"* Colorado thinks for a moment, then starts "Cindy." He vamps, then sings *"I wish I was an apple"* Stumpy: *"That's a good'n!"* *"Hangin' in a tree"* (Stumpy starts playing harmonica) *"and every time my sweetheart passed she'd take a bite of me."* This shot is quite long, so we can enjoy the three characters together.

22  Closeup of Colorado (closer than 5, since this song is more about him) *"She told me that she loved me, she called me sugar plum. She threw her arms around me. I thought my time had come."*

23  Medium shot of Stumpy in left foreground, Dude in the background to sing the chorus *"Get along home, Cindy Cindy, get along home Cindy, Cindy, get along home Cindy Cindy, I'll marry you some time."* They look at each other.

24  =22 Colorado: *"I wish I had a needle as fine as I could sew. I'd sew her in my pocket, and down the road I'd go. Cindy hugged and kissed me, she rung her hands and cried, and swore I was the prettiest thing that ever lived or died."*

25  Medium shot of Stumpy (slightly wider than 6) *"Get along home, Cindy Cindy, get along home Cindy Cindy"*

26  =1 Dude "*Get along home Cindy Cindy, I'll marry you*"

27  =25 Stumpy "*some time!*"

28  =7 Chance smiling while they hold the final note.

29  =end of 3, long shot of quartet. The repetition of this shot gives the
    sequence a rounded form, as does the repetition of shot 1 in 26, and that
    of Chance in shots 7 and 28. Other than those two, the shots in "Cindy"
    are taken from different angles from those in "Purple Light," emphasiz-
    ing very subtly the different moods of the two songs.

In "Purple Light," Colorado's gaze is always fixed on Dude, Dude switches
between the middle distance and Colorado, Stumpy switches between Colorado and Dude, and Chance, standing further apart, takes in the whole trio.
The song is symmetrical in its shot lengths: it begins with a lengthy shot of
Dude and ends with a lengthy shot of the trio. The second shot is of Chance,
and the second-to-last shot is of Stumpy, the two characters who have less
active roles in this first number. The shot lengths decrease into the alternating
motive section and increase again into the end of the song.

Wood says that "Cindy" comes across as "the 'feminine' response to
Dude's 'masculine' statement."[26] While there is some truth to this, especially
in the passive lyrics of "Cindy," Wood is not quite right when he says that
"throughout, Colorado appears to be singing to Dude." While he certainly is
in the first song, in the second his gaze seems directed at no one in particular.
Because of this, Nelson's performance in "Cindy" is less dramatically interesting than in what he does in "Purple Light." In the first song he is more a
part of the musical community, while in the second he is more the soloist:
Ricky Nelson the pop singer threatens to take over from Colorado the
cowboy. "Cindy" also has much less editing (eight shots as opposed to 21 in
"Purple Light"). Most of the "Purple Light" shots are the same medium closeups of Dude and Colorado (first seen in shots 4 and 5). Dude is in the frame
alone in eight shots, some of them held longer than most. Colorado is in the
frame alone for seven, although all are shorter than Dude's. Dude dominates
this first song musically and filmically. Colorado dominates "Cindy" in a
similar way: he is alone in two shots, but they are the two lengthiest in the
sequence. Dude and Stumpy have one solo shot each, plus they share one
shot, and Chance has one shot alone. The lengthiest shot of the sequence (21)
is the three-shot that ends "My Rifle," has transitional dialogue, and begins
"Cindy." The pillars of the whole sequence are Dude alone (1), this middle
transitional shot of the three musicians (21), and the final group shot. Hawks
takes us from one character to three, and finally all four, in a metaphor for
community building: one person brings in others, then finally all work
together to achieve harmony.

This quartet represents four different types of musical masculinity. The
only one who fits the traditional stereotype of manliness (i.e., to *not* be

musical) is Chance: he can enjoy listening to music up to a point, but music is something for people weaker than he to actually produce. In the song scene he seems to be regarding his colleagues' musicking the same way he would look on if they were doing any other sort of group activity. This is consistent with the Wayne persona: an occasional music listener but no enthusiast and certainly no joiner. In fact, at the end of the film when his love interest Feathers (Angie Dickinson) is about to sing, Chance tells her not to. Unlike Frank Morgan/Bogart in *To Have and Have Not*, who revels in Marie/Bacall's singing, Chance/Wayne is simply not interested, shifting attention to what Feathers is wearing rather than wanting to hear her perform (her former profession), no matter how she is dressed. Even in the emotional "Degüello" scene just before the song scene, the music seems to have no effect on Chance, who is focused entirely on Dude and the bottle of whiskey. There is not even any indication that Chance notices the music at all. When the "Degüello" is first heard about half way through the film, Chance only takes note when Colorado mentions it to him, and only displays any interest when he is told what the music *means* (i.e., no quarter for the soldiers holed up in the Alamo). He has no time for music as music. Music is just another activity to pass the time, not something to be one's focus. Hawks made a telling comment about this in his interview with Joseph McBride: he shot a scene for *El Dorado* (1966) in which Robert Mitchum sang, but Hawks's son said, "Dad, a sheriff shouldn't sing" so Hawks cut the scene.[27] Hawks obviously agreed with his son: singing is only for deputies, not sheriffs.[28]

Stumpy does notice the "Degüello" playing in the whiskey scene, but does not fully understand its significance. He goes to shut the window, but Dude stops him. For Stumpy, music is, and should only be, fun. He feels himself unable to sing during Dude and Colorado's performance of "My Rifle, My Pony and Me," although he is clearly enjoying it ("that's real pretty") and playing his harmonica for occasional support. He asks them to play something he can sing with them, and Colorado chooses the up-beat "Cindy." Stumpy sings along (badly) and plays his harmonica (better). For Stumpy, music is most enjoyable when it is participatory, a group activity, and when it is not emotional. Stumpy feels things deeply, but is not comfortable with his feelings: he deflects his respect for Dude after the whiskey scene through humor. Stumpy seems to recognize the valuable social function that music can have, although he is not comfortable with the stronger or negative emotions it can arouse.

In stark contrast to Stumpy and the amusical Chance is Dude, who fully recognizes and acknowledges the emotional power of music. His sensitivity is shown most clearly when the music he hears is what allows him to stop drinking, and when he chooses a lyrical song to sing in the next scene. Dude, like most other singing cowboys, manages to retain both his musicality and his masculinity. Brett explains that "though it is not proscribed in the same way as homosexuality, music has often been considered a dangerous substance, an agent of moral ambiguity always in danger of bestowing deviant status upon its practitioners."[29] This danger is avoided by Dude and the filmmakers because his use of music is clearly helping him find the opposite of danger and immorality as he decides he does not need to drink. Music also has a clear purpose as a social unifier, and the song scene can be read (like the choruses in *Red River*) as an example of the Western genre's portrayal of the formation of modern society through metaphorical means. Music-making is a concise and pleasurable way to demonstrate this to an audience. Of course, Dean Martin's own persona has a role to play as well, as audiences would have expected him to sing in this film as he had in most of his previous ones.

Colorado is the film's musicologist (and in fact offers a more accurate and positive portrait of the profession than Professor Frisbee in *A Song Is Born*). He is the only one of the four who knows the history of the "Degüello," and he is able to read its significance at the present moment. He is also able to choose the right song for Stumpy to sing with him and Dude, also joining in with Dude in "My Rifle" and later whistling the "Rio Bravo" theme song together with him to relieve tension straight after the film's climactic shootout with the Burdette gang. Colorado is familiar with American musical history and repertoire, approaching music-making as a participant observer. One can almost imagine him collecting songs from his fellow cowboys, adding them to his repertoire and increasingly able to choose the right song for the right context, as he chose "Cindy" for Stumpy. Colorado seems highly musically able; it appears that he is learning "My Rifle" as Dude sings it, first trying out the guitar chords and then joining in the singing. This mirrors his quickness with his gun. While Chance does not rate musicality very highly, music is yet another way in which his deputy Colorado is "good," that all-important Hawksian quality.

In film theorist Peter Wollen's words about Hawks's films, "the group members are bound together by rituals [...] and express themselves univocally in communal sing-songs."[30] But are they really "univocal?" In the case of *Bringing Up Baby* and *Only Angels Have Wings*, the heterogeneity of the vocal groups is foregrounded: the interspecies harmony sung by David, Susan, George, and Baby, and the singing with instruments of Geoff and Bonnie. In *To Have and Have Not*, Marie adds something (her voice) to Cricket's performance that helps him complete his song. In *Rio Bravo*, teen idol Ricky Nelson, crooner Dean Martin, and old-timer Walter Brennan each bring their own very different musical styles to the community. These Hawksian groups are not about giving up one's personal identity to join a community action that will lead to a glorious collective future, but are rather about pulling from the strengths of each group member to create a better present. Hawks's protagonists are all individualists. We may or may not agree with this essentially libertarian ideology, but Hawks gives a unique example of how music can play an important role in the ideology machine of narrative film.

## Notes

1  RKO acquired the rights to the song at the last minute, for $1000 (Gerald Mast, ed., *Bringing Up Baby* [New Brunswick, NJ: Rutgers University Press, 1988], 6).

2  The leopard could be seen as representing David to Susan – tame, but a wild animal nonetheless – or Susan to David – a tricky feline; perhaps the answer is both.

3  Mast, *Bringing Up Baby*, 142.

4  Mast, 223–224.

5  Peter Swaab, *Bringing Up Baby* (London: Palgrave Macmillan, 2010).

6  Bruce Kawin, ed., *To Have and Have Not* (Madison: University of Wisconsin Press, 1980), 87.

7  Kawin describes this scene in detail, 44–46.

8  Kawin, 200.

9  Kawin, 142.

10  For example, on *Bringing Up Baby* Walter Catlett as Constable Slocum was kept on set by having more scenes written for him. In addition to being friends with Hawks he was helping to coach Katharine Hepburn on comedy timing (Todd McCarthy, *The Grey Fox of Hollywood* [New York: Grove Press, 1997], 251).

11  Kawin, *To Have and Have Not*, 169. For a shot-by-shot breakdown of this sequence see Chapter 4.

12  Robin Wood enumerates some of these similarities.

> To restore the main plot-line of *To Have and Have Not* to that of *Casablanca*, all that is necessary is to eliminate the Lauren Bacall character and have Bogart in love with Madame de Bursac [the wife of the French Resistance fighter].
> "To Have (Written) and Have Not (Directed),"
> *Film Comment* 9, no. 3 (1973), 34

13  Kawin, *To Have and Have Not*, 48.

14  Wood, "To Have (Written) and Have Not (Directed)," 34.

15  Robin Wood, *Rio Bravo* (London: British Film Institute, 2003).

16  Gerald Mast, *Howard Hawks, Storyteller* (New York: Oxford University Press, 1982), 359–360.

17  Mast, 360.

18  The "Degüello," or "cutthroat song," is supposedly the trumpet call played by the Mexican army during the taking of the Alamo. The version in the film was composed by Tiomkin (Kathryn Kalinak, "Scoring the West: Dimitri Tiomkin and Howard Hawks," in Ian Brookes, ed., *Howard Hawks: New Perspectives* (London: British Film Institute, 2016).

19  Wood *Rio Bravo*, 73.

20  Wood, 74.

21  Philip Brett, "Piano Four-Hands: Schubert and the Performance of Gay Male Desire," *19th-Century Music* 21, no. 2 (1997); Philip Brett, "Musicality, Essentialism, and the Closet," in *Queering the Pitch*, ed. Philip Brett, Elizabeth Wood, and Gary C. Thomas, 2nd edition (New York: Routledge, 2006).

22  David Arnold, "My Rifle, My Pony, and Feathers: Music and the Making of Men in Howard Hawks' *Rio Bravo*," *Quarterly Review of Film and Video* 23, no. 3 (2006), 267–279.

23  Arnold, 271.

24  Arnold, 273.

25  Murphy directed only two films, but was an Academy Award-nominated screenwriter. He wrote two early Elia Kazan films, *Boomerang!* and *Panic in the Streets*,

being nominated for the former (his other nominated screenplay was 1953's *The Desert Rats*).

26  Wood *Rio Bravo*, 71.
27  Joseph McBride, *Hawks on Hawks*. (Lexington: University of Kentucky Press, 2013), 159.
28  Of course other men in powerful roles in Hawks's films, like Geoff in *Only Angles Have Wings*, do sing. There seems to be something about the Wild West that relegates singing to men without as much power.
29  Brett 2006, 11. This can apply not only to homosexuality but to femininity as well.
30  Quoted in Mast *Bringing Up Baby*, 272.

# Conclusion

The preceding five chapters have explored various facets of Howard Hawks's sonic style, especially his foregrounding of songs. But what happens to music in its absence? Hawks's early sound films, while not using much music, as was standard in the early 1930s, do generally adhere to the convention of having an overture and exit music over the opening and end credits. *The Crowd Roars* (1932), the story of race car driver Joe Greer (James Cagney) and the choice he must make between his girlfriend and his duty to his kid brother, breaks with both traditions, replacing these typically musical moments with the sound of automobiles. The first sound we hear is the racing cars' engines, playing under the Warner Bros. shield; we then see some action shots of a car crash, and only after the crowd roars in response to the crash do the traditional overture and opening credits begin. This technique of delaying the opening credits was surprisingly rare at that time, so this opening stands out as especially unusual. Aside from the opening credits the film has almost no music at all, apart from a brief bit of stock footage of a marching band at the big climactic race. Then, perhaps even more unusual than the delayed opening credits music, there is no final orchestral flourish at the end. We hear only the sound of the ambulance taking Joe to the hospital. The sound of automobile engines is, in Michel Chion's coinage, this film's "fundamental noise."[1] They replace a musical score in the film's soundscape, lying in the background of many scenes.

The film's other non-musical music is James Cagney's voice. Cagney's influential position at the beginning of the talkies is still somewhat under-rated. Comparing his vocal performance to those of other early talking film stars shows how groundbreaking he was. He speaks faster and with a greater variation of pitch than many of his contemporaries, taking advantage of the new sound recording techniques. The musicality of his speech makes his films more accessible to modern audiences than others of this period, even Hawks's own *Dawn Patrol*, in which the actors use a more theatrical style of speech. By the time Hawks made *Twentieth Century* in 1934 the new Cagney style had taken hold enough that John Barrymore could satirize this earlier theatrical style. Although Cagney's performances can seem mannered today, they are mannered in a more accessible way than those of many other early sound actors. Cagney seems to influence his fellow actors: compare Ann Dvorak's mode of speech in *Scarface* (1932) vs. *The Crowd Roars*.[2] In the later film she speaks in a more contemporary style (aside from in her moment of greatest weeping emotion, where she shows that she has not quite banished exaggerated theatricality). Joan Blondell also looks ahead stylistically, but Eric Linden's antiquated performance as Cagney's kid brother Eddie looks backward: the contrast is very telling and is a prime example of the rapid changes that were happening in film acting in the early 1930s.

The racing sequences show very clearly how these earlier films worked without music: where later films score such action scenes with rapidly shifting musical material to help the audience make sense of their continuity (see, for example, Pixar's *Cars* [2006] or the vehicle chase sequences of Christopher Nolan's *Dark Knight* trilogy [2005–2012]), *The Crowd Roars* relies solely on the sound of the engines and the commentary from the loudspeaker to make sense of the sequences. Alain Masson argues that it is only the commentator's voice who humanizes the action sequences; without this acousmêtre to tie them together, they would merely seem like disconnected images of cars and smoke.[3] *The Crowd Roars* offers no tunes for the audience to go out humming, but perhaps the fundamental noise of the automobiles, with Cagney's fluid vocal performance above it, is analogous to an early seventeenth-century monody with its bass accompaniment. The film is an excellent example of the sonic experimentation that was going on in the 1926–1932 transitional period, because filmmakers had no choice *but* to experiment. Each month brought new technological developments, and each released film brought new audience expectations of what the talkies could do. Hawks fully explored these sonic developments throughout his career, using music, dialogue, and sound effects in consistently creative ways.

Howard Hawks famously wanted his films to be "fun," both for him and his colleagues to make and for his audiences to watch. The result is that the films rarely challenge their audiences with structural or stylistic innovations. His camera remains mostly at eye level, his cutting is kept to a minimum and follows the standard practices of the time, he rarely uses voiceover, flashbacks, or other narrative tricks, and his script construction focuses on causal relationships and character motivations that are played out across the course of the film. The fun comes in watching attractive people doing exciting things, and his films that are generally considered less successful fall short on the character attraction side: *Land of the Pharaohs* features the exciting building of a pyramid, but the characters are not interesting. *Red Line 7000*, in spite of its many car racing sequences, features dull, interchangeable characters. In spite of its World War I action, *The Road to Glory* seems mostly miscast, with lead actors who lack charisma. The films that divide critics are argued by some to feature dull events: *Hatari!* is either a marvelous hang out with some fascinating characters, or a boring film that is mostly talk and little action. *Man's Favorite Sport?* is either a nice way to spend two hours with Rock Hudson and Paula Prentiss, or a boring slog through a fishing expedition. Hawks's films rarely make strong ideological points, and instead quietly convey Hawks's essentially libertarian philosophy. To be ideological or to push a message would not be "fun." Witness Hawks's criticisms of *High Noon* (1952), which he allegedly sought to answer in *Rio Bravo*: Zinnemann's "message movie" not only conveyed a questionable message but did it in a style that was not fun.

Manny Farber colorfully summarizes the groups that lie at the center of Hawks's films as "the creations of a man who is as divorced from modern *angst* as Fats Waller and whose whole movie-making system seems a secret preoccupation with linking, a connections business involving people, plots, and eight-inch hat brims."[4] The sense of fun that Hawks attempted to engender carries over into the music his characters use, and Farber's comparison of Hawks to Fats Waller is not too far off. Hawks's films rarely challenge their audiences musically, like Waller's songs, but both artists keep their audiences on the edge of their seats, wondering what exciting event or line of dialogue, or what virtuosic piano run will happen next. None of the films have scores that are as dissonant as Franz Waxman's for *Sunset Boulevard* or *A Place in the Sun*, or as experimental as Bernard Herrmann's for his films with Alfred Hitchcock, or even as overtly melodramatic as Frank Skinner's music for Douglas Sirk. Mostly (some of the Tiomkin films aside) the scores are unobtrusive and rather innocuous. As the foregoing has demonstrated, the films' most memorable musical moments are usually diegetic, serving outward characterization rather than inner psychology. Music is *used* by characters to tell each other something about themselves, or to cement social groups together. What all of Hawks's music has in common is that it is a form of communication.

## Notes

1 Michel Chion, *Film: A Sound Art* (New York: Columbia University Press, 2009).
2 Although both films were released in 1932, *Scarface* had been finished earlier and had a drawn-out postproduction process, in part due to issues of censorship (see Todd McCarthy, *Howard Hawks: The Grey Fox of Hollywood* [New York: Grove Press, 1997], 122–155).
3 Alain Masson, "Une beauté simple (La foule en délire)," *Positif* 240 (1981): 70–71.
4 Manny Farber, "Howard Hawks," in *Farber On Film*, ed. Robert Polito (New York: Library of America, 2009).

# Appendix
## Hawks Musico-Filmography

The data here were drawn from McCarthy and Mast's filmographies, corroborated by the American Film Institute Catalogue.[1] This list demonstrates that Hawks was very prolific not only as a director and producer, but also as a screenwriter and story writer, often in films' developmental stages, throughout his career. This inventory of films also shows that even in our age of streaming and "long tail" distribution, a large amount of Hollywood product, especially pre-1950, still remains commercially unavailable and hard to see. Warner Bros. has been the most proactive studio in releasing their back catalog, which includes films from Warners, MGM, and RKO. Data on silent film availability comes from the Library of Congress's American Silent Film Database. Hawks was involved in various capacities with a number of other films, either in production or development, especially in the early part of his career. This list includes only those films on which Hawks was credited, which he discussed in interviews, or for which material exists in his papers held at Brigham Young University. Titles in bold type are commonly regarded as "Hawks" films, even if he was not the sole credited director.

### 1917
*The Little Princess*
Mary Pickford Film Corp, dir. Marshall Neilan, uncredited assistant director Howard Hawks
Not commercially available, but see www.youtube.com/watch?v=zBCsD7 xnNVU.

### 1919
*His Night Out* **(And Three to Five Other One-Reel Monty Banks Comedies)**
According to McCarthy, drawing from interviews with Hawks, Hawks directed some of these.[2]
They do not appear in the AFI Catalogue. Lost films.

**1920**

### *Go and Get It*
dir. Marshall Neilan, co-producer Howard Hawks
According to McCarthy, Hawks was involved as a co-producer of this and the
  other listed films between 1920 and 1923.[3]
Copy in Cineteca Italiana.

### *Dinty*
dir. Marshall Neilan, co-producer Howard Hawks
Copy in Filmmuseum Amsterdam.

### *The Forbidden Thing*
dir. Allan Dwan, co-producer Howard Hawks
Lost film.

**1921**

### *A Perfect Crime*
dir. Allan Dwan, co-producer Howard Hawks
Lost film.

### *Man-Woman-Marriage*
dir. Allen Holubar, co-producer Howard Hawks
Copy in Filmmuseum Amsterdam.

### *Bob Hampton of Placer*
dir. Marshall Neilan, co-producer Howard Hawks
Lost film.

### *A Broken Doll*
dir. Allan Dwan, co-producer Howard Hawks
Copy in New Zealand Film Archive (repatriated to Library of Congress).

### *Bits of Life*
dir. Marshall Neilan, co-producer Howard Hawks
Lost film.

**1922**

### *The Lotus Eater*
dir. Marshall Neilan, co-producer Howard Hawks
The AFI gives January 1922 as release date, the Library of Congress
  December 1921.
Lost film.

### *Penrod*
dir. Marshall Neilan, co-producer Howard Hawks
Lost film.

**Fools First**
dir. Marshall Neilan, co-producer Howard Hawks
Lost film.

**Hurricane's Gal**
dir. Allen Holubar, co-producer Howard Hawks
Copies in Archives du Film du CNC, Gosfilmofond Moscow, Cineteca Italiana.

**Minnie**
dir. Marshall Neilan, co-producer Howard Hawks
Lost film.

## 1923

**Slander the Woman**
dir. Allan Holubar, co-producer Howard Hawks
Lost film.

**Quicksands**
Agfar Corp, dir. Jack Conway, producer and story Howard Hawks
Lost film.

## 1924

**Tiger Love**
Paramount, dir. George Melford, co-scenarist Howard Hawks
Based on the opera *El Gato Montes* by Manuel Penella, adapted from the English version which played in New York in 1921, *The Wild Cat*.[4] One might imagine that the cinema musicians played themes from the opera, at least in New York where it would have been familiar.
Lost film.

## 1925

**The Dressmaker from Paris**
Paramount, dir. Paul Bern, story Howard Hawks
Lost film.

## 1926

**The Road to Glory**
Fox, dir. Howard Hawks, original story Howard Hawks
Lost film.

**Honesty – The Best Policy**
Fox, dir. Chester Bennett, story Howard Hawks
Lost film.

### Fig Leaves
Fox, dir. Howard Hawks, original story Howard Hawks
Not commercially available, but see https://archive.org/details/FigLeaves.

## 1927
### The Cradle Snatchers
Fox, dir. Howard Hawks
Partially lost (some reels in Library of Congress).

### Paid to Love
Fox, dir. Howard Hawks
Not commercially available, but see www.dailymotion.com/video/x21j6t4.

### Underworld
Paramount, dir. Josef von Sternberg, uncredited co-scenarist Howard Hawks
McCarthy is skeptical of Hawks's claims to have been involved in the development of the film.[5]
Available on DVD from the Criterion Collection (*3 Silent Classics by Josef von Sternberg*), out of print as of this writing.

## 1928
### A Girl in Every Port
Fox, dir. Howard Hawks, original story Howard Hawks
Not commercially available, but see www.youtube.com/watch?v=Iu-Rpe8x3vo.

### Fazil
Fox, dir. Howard Hawks
Music: synchronized score by Erno Rapee, arranged by Roxy Rothafel.
Not commercially available, but see https://ok.ru/video/1265264102032.

### The Air Circus
Fox, dir. Howard Hawks and Lewis Seiler (dialogue sequences)
Music: anonymous synchronized score
Lost film.

## 1929
### Trent's Last Case
Fox, dir. Howard Hawks
Music: anonymous synchronized score
Copy (missing one reel) in Library of Congress.

## 1930
### The Dawn Patrol
First National, dir. Howard Hawks, co-scenarist Howard Hawks
Music: Leo Forbstein (conductor), "Poor Butterfly" (M. Raymond Hubbell); "How Stands the Glass," "Plum and Apple" (traditional)

Many filmographies, including McCarthy's, cite Forbstein and other studio music directors as composers of these early films' scores, but in reality it is unlikely that they were actually involved in the composition. The anonymous studio staff composers, arrangers, and orchestrators actually wrote most of the music. That the early Academy Awards were given to a studio's music director rather than the primary composer exacerbates the misunderstanding.

Available on DVD from Warner Archive Collection in an excellent print, and also on iTunes.

### Morocco

Paramount, dir. Josef von Sternberg, uncredited co-scenarist Howard Hawks

Music: "Give Me the Man Who Does Things," "What Am I Bid for My Apples?" Karl Hajos and Leo Robin.

Mast claims Hawks's involvement.[6] McCarthy does not mention it.

Available on Blu-Ray and DVD from the Criterion Collection (*Dietrich and von Sternberg in Hollywood*), and on DVD from Universal.

## 1931

### The Criminal Code

Columbia, dir. Howard Hawks

Music: none credited (only stock music for credits)

Available in a TCM/Warner DVD box set, *Karloff: Criminal Kind* (with *The Guilty Generation* and *Behind the Mask*).

## 1932

### Scarface

United Artists, dir. Howard Hawks

Music: Adolph Tandler, Gus Arnheim, music directors; "Some of These Days," "Wreck of the Old 97," sextet from *Lucia di Lammermoor*.

Available on DVD from Universal and on iTunes, and on a Blu-Ray bundled with the 4K Blu-Ray release of Brian De Palma's 1983 remake.

### The Crowd Roars

First National, dir. Howard Hawks, story Howard Hawks

Music: Leo F. Forbstein, music director

Available on DVD from Warner Archive Collection and on iTunes.

### Tiger Shark

First National, dir. Howard Hawks

Music: Leo Forbstein, music director, "Abdul Abulbul Amir" (traditional), Portuguese wedding music.

Available on DVD from Warner Archive Collection.

### Red Dust

MGM, dir. Victor Fleming, uncredited co-scenarist Howard Hawks

Mast makes an unsubstantiated claim about Hawks's involvement.[7] McCarthy relates a story in which Hawks was jealous of the film's success.[8]

Available on DVD from Warner Archive Collection, and on iTunes.

### Shanghai Express

MGM, dir. Josef von Sternberg, uncredited co-scenarist Howard Hawks

Mast claims Hawks's involvement, but as with *Morocco* it is not mentioned by McCarthy.[9]

Available on Blu-Ray and DVD from the Criterion Collection (*Dietrich and von Sternberg in Hollywood*), and on DVD from Universal.

## 1933

### The Prizefighter and the Lady

MGM, dir. W.S. Van Dyke, film begun by Howard Hawks

Music: Frank Skinner, Paul Marquardt, arrangers; "Downstream Drifter" (David Snell) sung onscreen by Myrna Loy (dubbed by Bernice Alstock); "Lucky Fella" (Jimmy McHugh and Dorothy Fields) performed by Max Baer and a chorus line.

Available on DVD from Warner Archive Collection.

### Today We Live

MGM, dir. and producer Howard Hawks

Music: uncredited title music by William Axt (according to IMDB); "Poor Butterfly" (M. Raymond Hubbell); "The Young Observer"

Available on DVD from Warner Archive Collection.

## 1934

### Viva Villa!

MGM, dir. Jack Conway, film begun by Howard Hawks

Music: Herbert Stothart, musical consultant Juan Aguilar; a variety of source music including Mendelssohn's wedding march and "Cucuracha"

Available on DVD from Warner Archive Collection.

### Twentieth Century

Columbia, dir. and producer Howard Hawks

Music: Uncredited (opening and closing credits only)

Available on DVD from Sony (out of print) and on iTunes.

## 1935
### *Barbary Coast*
Goldwyn, dir. Howard Hawks

Music: Alfred Newman; extensive traditional music used as source music and in the score, including "I Dream of Jeannie," "Oh Susannah," and "Hearts and Flowers"

Available on DVD from Warner Archive Collection.

### *Ceiling Zero*
First National, dir. Howard Hawks

Music: Leo Forbstein, music director; a small amount of source music, including "I Can't Give You Anything But Love, Baby"

Available on DVD from Warner Bros. France (*Brumes*).

## 1936
### *The Road to Glory*
Fox, dir. Howard Hawks

Music: Louis Silvers, musical director; extensive use of Schubert's "Ave Maria" and French World War I music

Available on DVD from 20th Century Fox Cinema Archives, and from Opening (France), with bonus interviews, as *Les chemins de la gloire*.

### *Come and Get It*
Goldwyn, dir. Howard Hawks and William Wyler

Music: Alfred Newman, incorporating traditional songs such as "Aura Lee" and "Oh Susannah"

Available on DVD from Warner Archive Collection.

### *Sutter's Gold*
Universal, dir. James Cruze, uncredited co-scenarist Howard Hawks and William Faulkner (begun before *Barbary Coast*)

Music: Franz Waxman

Not commercially available.

## 1937
### *Captains Courageous*
MGM, dir. Victor Fleming, uncredited co-scenarist Howard Hawks

Unsubstantiated claim by Mast, who seems to believe Hawks's claim that he ghost-wrote many of Fleming's films and was instrumental in developing his career.[10]

Music: Franz Waxman; songs: "Ooh What a Terrible Man" and "Don't Cry Little Fish," Waxman and Gus Kahn; "Blow the Man Down" and "What Shall We Do with a Drunken Sailor;" traditional melodies with original Portuguese lyrics by Zacharias Yaconelli

Available on DVD from Warner Home Video.

**1938**

*Bringing Up Baby*

RKO, dir. and producer Howard Hawks

Music: Roy Webb; frequent use of "I Can't Give You Anything But Love, Baby" (Jimmy McHugh and Dorothy Fields)

Available on DVD from Warner Bros., with commentary by Peter Bogdanovich and documentaries on the filmmakers and stars. Also on iTunes.

*Test Pilot*

MGM, dir. Victor Fleming, uncredited co-scenarist Howard Hawks

Unsubstantiated claim by Mast (398).[11]

Music: Franz Waxman

Available on DVD from Warner Archive Collection.

**1939**

*Only Angels Have Wings*

Columbia, dir. and producer Howard Hawks, story Howard Hawks [uncredited]

Music: Dimitri Tiomkin; a large variety of source music, especially "Some of These Days," "The Peanut Vendor," "Liebestraum"

Available on DVD from Sony, and on Blu-Ray and DVD from the Criterion Collection. The Criterion edition is a 4K restoration, and includes relevant audio from the 1972 Bogdanovich interview with Hawks, an interview with David Thomson, the documentary *Howard Hawks and His Aviation Movies*, and the 1939 Lux Radio Theatre adaptation. Also on iTunes.

*Gone With the Wind*

Selznick, dir. Victor Fleming, uncredited co-scenarist Howard Hawks

Another unsubstantiated Hawks/Mast claim.

Music: Max Steiner

Available on Blu-Ray and DVD from Warner Home Video.

*Gunga Din*

RKO, dir. George Stevens, uncredited co-scenarist Howard Hawks

Music: Alfred Newman

Available on DVD from Warner Home Video.

*Indianapolis Speedway*

Warner Bros., dir. Lloyd Bacon, story Howard Hawks

There is no record of Hawks's direct involvement with this remake of *The Crowd Roars*.

Music: Adolph Deutsch

Not commercially available, but see https://ok.ru/video/371064965634.

**1940**

*His Girl Friday*

Columbia, dir. and producer Howard Hawks

Music: Morris Stoloff, musical director

Available on DVD from Sony, and on Blu-Ray and DVD from the Criterion Collection. The Criterion edition is an HD transfer, and includes relevant audio and video from the 1972 Bogdanovich and 1973 Schickel interviews with Hawks, an interview with David Bordwell, earlier featurettes (from the Sony DVD) on the film, Hawks, and Russell, the 1940 Lux Radio Theatre adaptation, as well as a 4K restoration of Lewis Milestone's *The Front Page* (1931).

*Murder in the Air*

Warner Bros., dir. Lewis Seiler, uncredited script development Howard Hawks

Music: Uncredited

Not commercially available, but see www.dailymotion.com/video/x59cv1q.

**1941**

*Sergeant York*

Warner Bros., dir. Howard Hawks

Music: Max Steiner; extensive quotations of World War I music ("Pack Up Your Troubles," "In the Army Now") and traditional songs ("Give Me That Old Time Religion," "Yankee Doodle")

Available on DVD from Warner Bros. in a special edition with documentaries, shorts, and a commentary by Jeanine Basinger. Also on iTunes. A suite from Steiner's score was recorded by the City of Prague Philharmonic, released on various compilations.

**1942**

*Ball of Fire*

Goldwyn, dir. Howard Hawks

Music: Alfred Newman, with important contributions from Gene Krupa and his big band ("Drum Boogie") and traditional music ("Sweet Genevieve" and "Gaudeamus Igitur")

Available on DVD from Warner Bros.

**1943**

*The Outlaw*

RKO, dir. Howard Hughes (who took over early in production from Howard Hawks)

Music: Victor Young

Available on Blu-Ray from Kino Lorber in a 2K restoration, with an audio commentary by Troy Howarth. Because the film has lapsed into public domain, may DVD releases exist, of mostly very poor transfers.

### Air Force
Warner Bros., dir. Howard Hawks
Music: Franz Waxman, with frequent quotations of "Up We Go"
Available on DVD from Warner Archive Collection. Also on iTunes.

### Corvette K-225
Universal, dir. Richard Rossen, producer Howard Hawks (also directed a few
  scenes)
Music: David Buttolph
Not commercially available, but see https://ok.ru/video/347755973283.

### For Whom the Bell Tolls
Paramount, dir. Sam Wood, uncredited co-scenarist Howard Hawks
Music: Victor Young, orch. George Parrish and Leo Shuken
Available on Blu-Ray and DVD from Universal.

## 1944
### To Have and Have Not
Warner Bros., dir. and producer Howard Hawks
Music: Max Steiner; extensive use of source music from Hoagy Carmichael
  ("How Little We Know" by Carmichael and Johnny Mercer; "Baltimore
  Oriel," "Hong Kong Blues")
Available on Blu-Ray and DVD from Warner Archive Collection. Includes a
  short documentary and the 1946 Lux Radio broadcast.

## 1946
### The Big Sleep
Warner Bros., dir. and producer Howard Hawks
Music: Max Steiner; popular source music, including a performance by
  Bacall of "And His Tears Flowed Like Wine" (Stan Kenton)
Available on Blu-Ray and DVD from Warner Archive Collection. Includes
  both the 1945 and 1946 versions, and a short documentary on the differ-
  ences between them. A suite of Steiner's score is available on various
  releases played by the National Symphony Orchestra conducted by Charles
  Gerhardt.

## 1947
### Moss Rose
Fox, dir. Gregory Ratoff, uncredited co-scenarist Howard Hawks (early in the
  film's development)
Music: David Buttolph
Available on DVD from Fox Cinema Archives.

**1948**
*Red River*
United Artists, dir. and producer Howard Hawks
Music: Dimitri Tiomkin; score incorporates traditional music
*Red River* has been very well served on Blu-Ray, with three separate editions. The most important of these is from Criterion, which includes 2K restorations of both versions of the film, interviews with Peter Bogdanovich, Molly Haskell, and Lee Clark Mitchell, excerpts from the 1972 Bogdanovich interview and an interview with Borden Chase, the 1949 Lux Radio Theatre adaptation, and a copy of the full novel by Chase. Wildside released a French version (*La Rivière rouge*), which also includes both versions of the film, plus a documentary on the differences and a book by Philippe Garnier, *Howard Hawks et la conquête du western*. Masters of Cinema released an edition in the UK, which only includes the long version but also an interview with Dan Sallitt and an isolated music-and-effects track. The full score was recorded by the Moscow Symphony Orchestra, conducted by William Stromberg, for Naxos.

*A Song Is Born*
Goldwyn, dir. Howard Hawks [remake of *Ball of Fire*]
Music: Emil Newman, Hugo Friedhofer; songs "A Song is Born" and "Daddy-O" by Don Raye and Gene DePaul; various source music from the jazz musicians
Available on DVD from Warner Archive Collection (part of the collection *Danny Kaye: The Golden Years*).

**1949**
*I Was a Male War Bride*
Fox, dir. Howard Hawks
Music: Cyril Mockridge
Available on DVD from Fox, and on a German Blu-Ray from Fox (*Ich War eine Männliche Kriegesbraut*). Also on iTunes.

**1951**
*The Thing from Another World*
RKO, dir. Christian Nyby, producer and screenplay Howard Hawks
Music: Dimitri Tiomkin
Available on Blu-Ray and DVD from Warner Bros. (Universal in the UK), and in a special edition from Editions Montparnasse with commentary and interviews (*La chose d'un autre monde*). Also on iTunes. The original soundtrack recording has been released by Film Score Monthly in a limited edition.

**1952**

*The Big Sky*

RKO, dir. and producer Howard Hawks

Music: Dimitri Tiomkin; a variety of source music, including Tiomkin's song "Quand je rêve"

Available on DVD from Editions Montparnasse (*La captive aux yeux clairs*). Includes both versions of the film and an interview with Todd McCarthy. Also available on iTunes. Brigham Young University has released the original soundtrack recording. A suite from the score was recorded for RCA by Charles Gerhardt and the National Symphony Orchestra.

*Monkey Business*

Fox, dir. Howard Hawks

Music: Leigh Harline; important dramatic use of "The Whiffenpoof Song" (Guy Scull)

Available on DVD from Fox, and on iTunes.

*O. Henry's Full House – "The Ransom of Red Chief"*

Fox, segment dir. Howard Hawks

Music: Alfred Newman

Available on DVD from Fox and on Blu-Ray from Koch Media (Germany; *Fünf Perlen*). The original soundtrack has been released on Kritzerland.

*Scandal Sheet*

Columbia, dir. Phil Karlson, Hawks was producer of an earlier planned version

Music: George Duning

Available on Blu-Ray from Powerhouse Films (in the collection *Samuel Fuller at Columbia*).

**1953**

*Gentlemen Prefer Blondes*

Fox, dir. Howard Hawks

Music: Lionel Newman, music director; songs by Jule Styne and Leo Robin ("Just Two Little Girls From Little Rock," "Diamonds Are a Girl's Best Friend"); Hoagy Carmichael and Harold Adamson ("Ain't There Anyone Here for Love?" "When Love Goes Wrong")

Available on Blu-Ray and DVD from Fox. Also on iTunes. The songs have been frequently released on LP and CD.

**1955**

*Land of the Pharaohs*

Warner Bros., dir. and producer Howard Hawks

Music: Dimitri Tiomkin

Available on DVD from Warner Archive Collection. Includes a commentary by Peter Bogdanovich. Film Score Monthly has released the original soundtrack, with bonus tracks. Elmer Bernstein recorded much of the score with the Royal Philharmonic Orchestra in 1978.

### The Left Hand of God
Fox, dir. Edward Dmytryk, early screenplay draft by Howard Hawks and William Faulkner
Music: Victor Young, orch. Edward Powell
Available on Blu-Ray from Rimini (France: *La main gauche du seigneur*), iTunes from Fox.

## 1957
### The Sun Also Rises
Fox, dir. Henry King, Hawks was producer of an earlier version
Music: Hugo Friedhofer, orch. Edward Powell
Available on DVD from Fox.

## 1959
### Rio Bravo
Warner Bros., dir. and producer Howard Hawks
Music: Dimitri Tiomkin, lyrics for "Purple Light" and "Rio Bravo" by Paul Francis Webster; prominent performance of traditional song "Cindy"
Available on Blu-Ray and DVD from Warner Bros. Includes commentary by John Carpenter and Richard Schickel, documentaries on the film, and Richard Schickel's 1973 documentary *The Man Who Made the Movies: Howard Hawks*. Also on iTunes. Intrada has released a special edition of the original soundtrack recordings. Dean Martin released versions of the film's songs.

## 1962
### Hatari!
Paramount, dir. and producer Howard Hawks
Music: Henry Mancini; song "Just for Tonight" by Hoagy Carmichael and Johnny Mercer
Available on Blu-Ray and DVD from Warner Bros., and on iTunes. RCA released the soundtrack with the release of the film. In 2012 Intrada produced a special edition of the soundtrack with bonus tracks.

## 1964
### Man's Favorite Sport?
Universal, dir. Howard Hawks
Music: Henry Mancini; title song by Mancini and Johnny Mercer
Available on Blu-Ray and DVD from Universal.

## 1965
### *Red Line 7000*
Paramount, dir. Howard Hawks

Music: Nelson Riddle, various source music ("Wildcat Jones" by Carol Connors and Buzz Cason, "Let Me Find Someone New" by Connors and Riddle)

Long unavailable, *Red Line 7000* was released on Blu-Ray in 2017 by Kino Lorber. Includes a commentary by Julie Kirgo and Nick Redman.

## 1967
### *El Dorado*
Paramount, dir. Howard Hawks

Music: Nelson Riddle; title song with lyrics by John Gabriel

Released on Blu-Ray and DVD by Paramount. Includes commentaries by Peter Bogdanovich and Richard Schickel, as well as documentaries on the film. Also on iTunes. Epic Records released the soundtrack contemporaneously with the film.

### *Casino Royale*
prod. Charles K. Feldman, dir. Joseph McGrath and others, uncredited developmental co-scenarist Howard Hawks

Music: Burt Bacharach

Songs: "Casino Royale," uncredited; "The Look of Love," Bacharach and Hal David

Available on Blu-Ray and DVD from MGM.

## 1970
### *Rio Lobo*
Cinema Center, dir. Howard Hawks

Music: Jerry Goldsmith

Available on Blu-Ray and DVD from Paramount. La-La Land released the original soundtrack in 2012.

## Notes

1 Todd McCarthy, *Howard Hawks: The Grey Fox of Hollywood* (New York: Grove Press, 1997), 667–690; Gerald Mast, *Howard Hawks, Storyteller* (New York: Oxford University Press, 1982), 390–398.
2 McCarthy, 50.
3 McCarthy, 52–56.
4 "The Wild Cat," *Washington Post*, June 29, 1924, A2.
5 McCarthy, 76.
6 Mast, 9.
7 Mast, 398.
8 McCarthy, 182.
9 Mast, 9.
10 Mast, 396.
11 Mast, 398.

# References

Altman, Rick. *The American Musical*. Bloomington: Indiana University Press, 1987.

Altman, Rick. *Silent Film Sound*. New York: Columbia University Press, 2004.

Anderson, Michael J. "Howard Hawks." In *Oxford Bibliographies*. Oxford University Press, 2011. Accessed July 26, 2018. http://oxfordbibliographies.com.

Arbuthnot, Lucie and Gail Seneca. "Pre-Text and Text in *Gentlemen Prefer Blondes*." In *Hollywood Musicals: The Film Reader*, edited by Steven Cohan. London: Routledge, 2002.

Arnold, David. "My Rifle, My Pony, and Feathers: Music and the Making of Men in Howard Hawks' *Rio Bravo*." *Quarterly Review of Film and Video* 23, no. 3 (2006): 267–279. doi: 10.1080/105092090503367.

Beach, Christopher. "Is Class Necessary? Preston Sturges and Howard Hawks in the Early 1940s." In *Class, Language, and American Film Comedy*. Cambridge: Cambridge University Press, 2002.

Bellour, Raymond. "The Obvious and the Code." *Screen* 15, no. 4 (1974), 7–17. doi: 10.1093/screen/15.4.7.

Berliner, Todd. *Hollywood Aesthetic: Pleasure in American Cinema*. New York: Oxford University Press, 2017.

Bogdanovich, Peter. Audio commentary to *Land of the Pharaohs*. Los Angeles: Warner Archive Collection, 2007. DVD.

Bogdanovich, Peter. "Bogdanovich on Red River." *Red River [1948]*. New York: Criterion Collection, no. 709 (2014). Blu-Ray.

Bogdanovich, Peter. "Hawks and Bogdanovich." *Red River [1948]*. New York: Criterion Collection, no. 709 (2014). Blu-Ray.

Bogdanovich, Peter. "Hawks on Hawks." *His Girl Friday [1940]*. New York: Criterion Collection, no. 849 (2017). Blu-Ray.

Bordwell, David. "My girl Friday, and his, and yours." *Observations on Film Art* (blog). January 16, 2017. www.davidbordwell.net/blog/2017/01/16/my-girl-friday-and-his-and-yours/. Accessed May 16, 2018.

Bordwell, David, Kristin Thompson, and Janet Staiger. *The Classical Hollywood Cinema: Film Style and Mode of Production to 1960*. New York: Columbia University Press, 1985.

Brett, Philip. "Piano Four-Hands: Schubert and the Performance of Gay Male Desire." *19th-Century Music* 21, no. 2 (1997), 149–176. doi: 10.2307/746896.

Brett, Philip. "Musicality, Essentialism, and the Closet." In *Queering the Pitch*, edited by Philip Brett, Elizabeth Wood, and Gary C. Thomas. 2nd edition. New York: Routledge, 2006.

Britton, Andrew. *Katharine Hepburn: Star as Feminist*. New York: Columbia University Press, 2003.

Brookes, Ian. "More than Just Dance Music: Hawks and Jazz in the 1940s." In *Howard Hawks: New Perspectives*. London: British Film Institute, 2016.

Brookes, Ian, ed. *Howard Hawks: New Perspectives*. London: British Film Institute, 2016.

Caps, John. *Henry Mancini: Reinventing Film Music*. Urbana: University of Illinois Press, 2012.

Chandler, Raymond. *The Big Sleep*. In *Raymond Chandler: Stories and Early Novels*. New York: Library of America, 1995.

Chion, Michel. *Film: A Sound Art*. Translated by Claudia Gorbman. New York: Columbia University Press, 2009.

Chion, Michel. *La musique au cinéma*. Paris: Fayard, 1995.

Cooke, Mervyn. *A History of Film Music*. Cambridge: Cambridge University Press, 2008.

Day, Kristen. *Cowboy Classics: The Roots of the American Western in the Epic Tradition*. Edinburgh: Edinburgh University Press, 2016.

DiBattista, Maria. *Fast-talking Dames*. New Haven, CT: Yale University Press, 2001.

Doty, Alexander. "Everyone's Here for Love: Bisexuality and *Gentlemen Prefer Blondes*." In *Flaming Classics: Queering the Film Canon*. London: Routledge, 2000.

Durkheim, Emile. *The Division of Labour in Society*. Translated by W.D. Halls. New York: Free Press, 1984.

Farber, Manny. "Howard Hawks." In *Farber on Film*, edited by Robert Polito. New York: Library of America, 2009.

Gabbard, Krin. *Jammin' at the Margins: Jazz and the American Cinema*. Chicago: University of Chicago Press, 1996.

Gossett, Philip. *Divas and Scholars: Performing Italian Opera*. Chicago: University of Chicago Press, 2006.

Guillem, Giordano. "Autopsie d'un montage." *La Rivière Rouge [1948]*. Paris: Wildside, 1000371489, 2013. Blu-Ray.

Hansen, Helen. *Hollywood Soundscapes: Film Sound Style, Craft and Production in the Classical Era*. London: Palgrave, 2017.

Haskell, Molly. *From Reverence to Rape: The Treatment of Women in the Movies*. 3rd edition. Chicago: University of Chicago Press, 2016.

Hillier, Jim and Peter Wollen, eds. *Howard Hawks: American Artist*. London: British Film Institute, 1996.

Jacobs, Lea. *Film Rhythm After Sound: Technology, Music, Performance*. Berkeley: University of California Press, 2015.

Kalinak, Kathryn. *How the West Was Sung: Music in the Westerns of John Ford*. Berkeley: University of California Press, 2007.

Kalinak, Kathryn. "Scoring the West: Dimitri Tiomkin and Howard Hawks." In *Howard Hawks: New Perspectives*, edited by Ian Brookes. London: British Film Institute, 2016.

Kawin, Bruce, ed. *To Have and Have Not.* Madison: University of Wisconsin Press, 1980.

Kolker, Robert. *Film, Form, and Culture.* New York: McGraw Hill, 2006.

Kozloff, Sarah. *Overhearing Film Dialogue.* Berkeley: University of California Press., 2000.

Larsen, Peter. *Film Music.* London: Reaktion, 2007.

Larsen, Peter. *Film Music.* London: Reaktion, 2007.

Levack, Chandler. "Ten Commandments of the Causal Hangout Movie." *MOTIF(F)* (blog). May 3, 2016. www.tiff.net/the-review/the-ten-commandments-of-the-casual-hangout-movie/. Accessed June 25, 2018.

Lewis, Hannah. *French Musical Culture and the Coming of Sound Cinema.* New York: Oxford University Press, 2019.

Liandrat-Guigues, Suzanne. *Red River.* London: British Film Institute, 2000.

Magee, Gayle Sherwood. *Altman's Soundtracks: Film, Music and Sound from "M\*A\*S\*H" to "A Prairie Home Companion."* New York: Oxford University Press, 2014.

Mancini, Henry and Gene Lees. *Did They Mention the Music?* New York: Cooper Square Press, 2001.

Masson, Alain. "Une beauté simple (La foule en délire)." *Positif* 240 (1981), 70–71.

Mast, Gerald. *Howard Hawks: Storyteller.* New York: Oxford University Press, 1982.

Mast, Gerald, ed. *Bringing Up Baby.* New Brunswick, NJ: Rutgers University Press, 1988.

McBride, Joseph. *Hawks on Hawks.* Lexington: University of Kentucky Press, 2013.

McCarthy, Todd. *Howard Hawks: The Grey Fox of Hollywood.* New York: Grove Press, 1997.

McQuiston, Kate. *We'll Meet Again: Musical Design in the Films of Stanley Kubrick.* New York: Oxford University Press, 2013.

Melnick, Ross. *American Showman: Samuel "Roxy" Rothafel and the Birth of the Entertainment Industry, 1908–1935.* New York: Columbia University Press, 2012.

Metz, Christian. *Impersonal Enunciation, or the Place of Film.* Translated by Cormac Deane. New York: Columbia University Press, 2016.

Meyer, Stephen C. *Epic Sound: Music in Postwar Hollywood Biblical Films.* Bloomington: Indiana University Press, 2015.

Morgan, John. Liner notes for Dimitri Tiomkin, *Red River.* Moscow Symphony Orchestra and Chorus. William Stromberg. Naxos 8.557699, 2003.

Mulvey, Laura. "*Gentlemen Prefer Blondes*: Anita Loos/Howard Hawks/Marilyn Monroe." In *Howard Hawks: American Artist,* edited by Jim Hillier and Peter Wollen. London: British Film Institute, 1996.

Neumeyer, David. "The Resonances of Wagnerian Opera and Nineteenth-Century Melodrama in the Film Scores of Max Steiner." In *Wagner and Cinema,* edited by Jeongwon Joe and Sander L. Gilman. Bloomington: Indiana University Press, 2010.

Neumeyer, David, James Buhler, and Rob Deemer. *Hearing Through Movies: Music and Sound in Film History.* New York: Oxford University Press, 2010.

Neumeyer, David and James Buhler. *Meaning and Interpretation of Music in Cinema.* Bloomington: University of Indiana Press, 2015.

Pierpont, Claudia Roth. "Katharine Hepburn: Woman of the Century." *Woman of the Year [1942].* New York: Criterion Collection, no. 867, 2017. Blu-Ray.

Pippin, Robert. *Hollywood Westerns and American Myth.* New Haven, CT: Yale University Press, 2010.

Platte, Nathan. *Making Music in Selznick's Hollywood.* New York: Oxford University Press, 2018.

Pogue, Leland. *Howard Hawks.* Boston: Twayne Publishers, 1982.

Powers, Harold. "'La solita forma' and 'The Uses of Convention.'" *Acta Musicologica* 59, no. 1 (1987): 65–90. doi: 10.2307/932865.

Previn, André. *No Minor Chords: My Days in Hollywood.* New York: Doubleday, 1991.

"Red River cue sheet." N.d. Dimitri Tiomkin: The Official Website. www.dimitri tiomkin.com/red-river-motion-picture-1948/red-river-cue-sheet/. Accessed July 4, 2018.

Rivette, Jacques. "The Genius of Howard Hawks." In *Howard Hawks: American Artist,* edited by Jim Hillier and Peter Wollen. London: British Film Institute, 1996 (orig. published 1956).

Rosenbaum, Jonathan. "Gold Diggers of 1953: Howard Hawks's *Gentlemen Prefer Blondes.*" In *Placing Movies: The Practice of Film Criticism.* Berkeley: University of California Press, 1995.

Said, Edward. *On Late Style.* New York: Pantheon Books, 2006.

Sarris, Andrew. *The American Cinema: Directors and Directions.* New York: Dutton, 1968.

Scheurer, Timothy E. *Music and Mythmaking in Film.* Jefferson, NC: McFarland and Company, 2008.

Shumway, David. "Screwball Comedies: Constructing Romance, Mystifying Marriage." *Cinema Journal* 30, no. 4 (1991): 7–23. doi: 10.2307/1224884.

Slowik, Michael. *After the Silents: Hollywood Film Music in the Early Sound Era, 1926–1934.* New York: Columbia University Press, 2014.

Small, Christopher. *Musicking.* Hanover, NH: University Press of New England, 1998.

Smith, Jeff. *Songs of Commerce: Marketing Popular Film Music.* New York: Columbia University Press, 1998.

Sullivan, Jack. *Hitchcock's Music.* New Haven, CT: Yale University Press, 2006.

Sutton, Donald. "Rituals of Smoking in Hollywood's Golden Age: Hawks, Furthman and the Ethnographic History of Film." *Film & History* 29, no. 3–4 (1999): 70–85.

Swaab, Peter. *Bringing Up Baby.* London: Palgrave Macmillan, 2010.

Thomas, Tony. *Films of the 40s.* New York: Carol, 1990.

Thomson, David. *The Big Sleep.* London: British Film Institute, 1997.

Waterbucket. "Quentin Tarantino about 'Rio Bravo' – 2007." *YouTube.* www.youtube.com/watch?v=KjX010pdIro. Accessed June 28, 2018.

Wierzbicki, James. *Film Music: A History.* New York: Routledge, 2009.

Wierzbicki, James, ed. *Music, Sound and Filmmakers: Sonic Styles in Cinema.* New York: Routledge, 2012.

Wilkins, Heidi. *Talkies, Road Movies, and Chick Flicks.* Edinburgh: Edinburgh University Press, 2016.

Wright, Ellen. "'A Travesty on Sex': Gender and Performance in *Gentlemen Prefer Blondes.*" In *Howard Hawks: American Artist.* edited by Jim Hillier and Peter Wollen. London: British Film Institute, 1996.

Wollen, Peter. *Signs and Meaning in the Cinema*. 3rd ed. London: British Film Institute, 2013.

Wood, Robin. *Howard Hawks*. 3rd ed. Detroit, MI: Wayne State University Press, 2006.

Wood, Robin. *Rio Bravo*. London: British Film Institute, 2003.

Wood, Robin. "To Have (Written) and Have Not (Directed)." *Film Comment* 9, no. 3 (1973), 30–35.

Zamecnik, J.S. and Harry D. Kerr. "Neapolitan Nights." New York: Sam Fox Pub. Co., 1926.

# Index

Printed in the United States
by Baker & Taylor Publisher Services